TOKYO RESTAURANT DESIGN COLLECTION 2007

最新レストランの空間デザイン集 2007

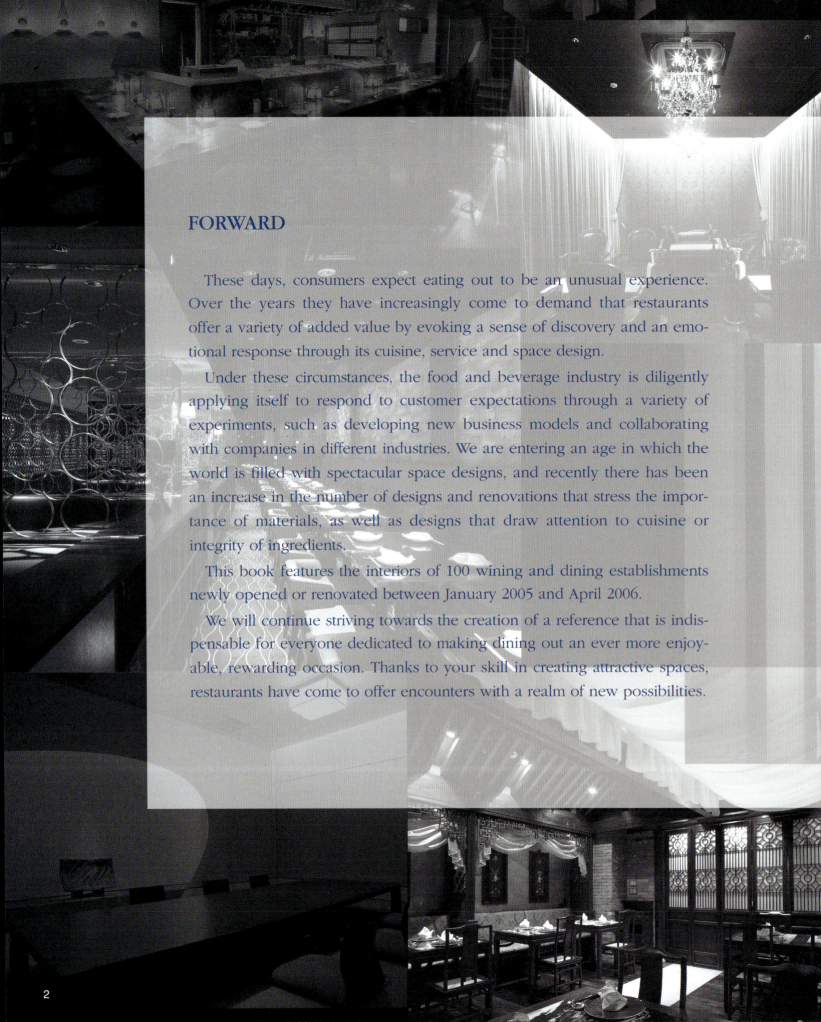

FORWARD

These days, consumers expect eating out to be an unusual experience. Over the years they have increasingly come to demand that restaurants offer a variety of added value by evoking a sense of discovery and an emotional response through its cuisine, service and space design.

Under these circumstances, the food and beverage industry is diligently applying itself to respond to customer expectations through a variety of experiments, such as developing new business models and collaborating with companies in different industries. We are entering an age in which the world is filled with spectacular space designs, and recently there has been an increase in the number of designs and renovations that stress the importance of materials, as well as designs that draw attention to cuisine or integrity of ingredients.

This book features the interiors of 100 wining and dining establishments newly opened or renovated between January 2005 and April 2006.

We will continue striving towards the creation of a reference that is indispensable for everyone dedicated to making dining out an ever more enjoyable, rewarding occasion. Thanks to your skill in creating attractive spaces, restaurants have come to offer encounters with a realm of new possibilities.

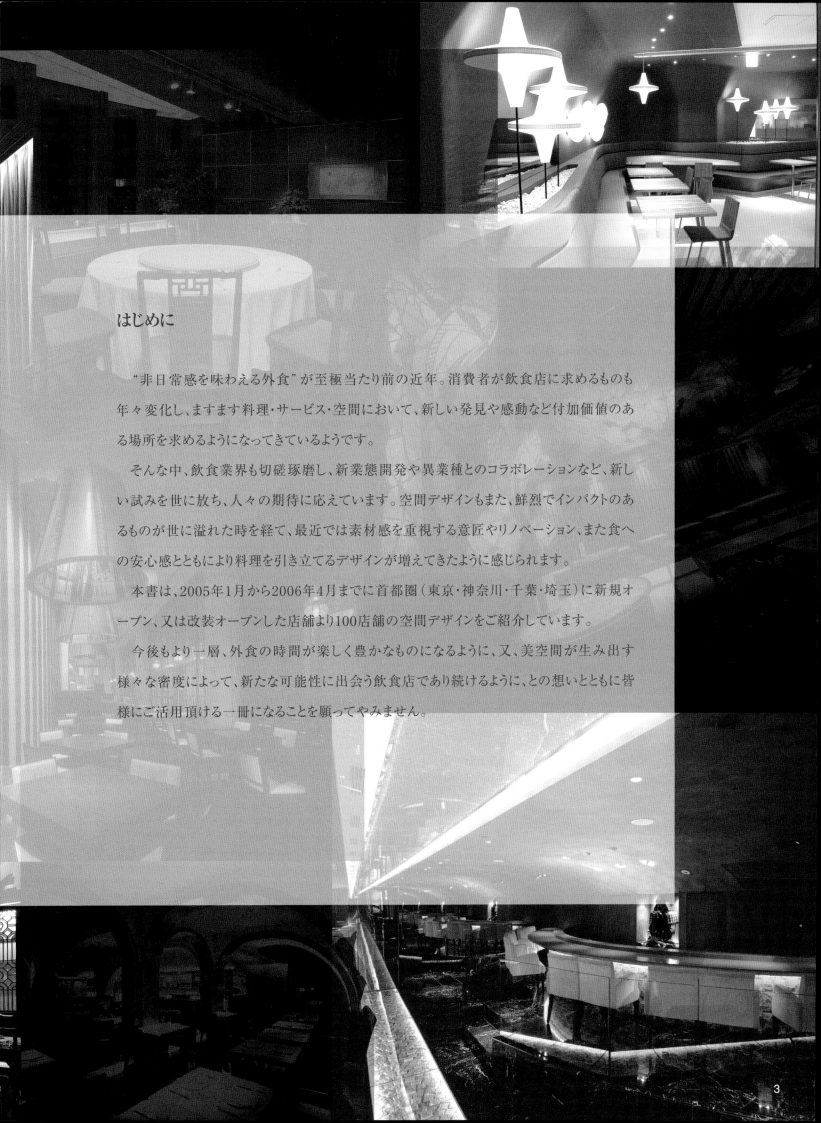

はじめに

　"非日常感を味わえる外食" が至極当たり前の近年。消費者が飲食店に求めるものも年々変化し、ますます料理・サービス・空間において、新しい発見や感動など付加価値のある場所を求めるようになってきているようです。

　そんな中、飲食業界も切磋琢磨し、新業態開発や異業種とのコラボレーションなど、新しい試みを世に放ち、人々の期待に応えています。空間デザインもまた、鮮烈でインパクトのあるものが世に溢れた時を経て、最近では素材感を重視する意匠やリノベーション、また食への安心感とともにより料理を引き立てるデザインが増えてきたように感じられます。

　本書は、2005年1月から2006年4月までに首都圏（東京・神奈川・千葉・埼玉）に新規オープン、又は改装オープンした店舗より100店舗の空間デザインをご紹介しています。

　今後もより一層、外食の時間が楽しく豊かなものになるように、又、美空間が生み出す様々な密度によって、新たな可能性に出会う飲食店であり続けるように、との想いとともに皆様にご活用頂ける一冊になることを願ってやみません。

CONTENTS

1 JAPANESE RESTAURANTS

日本料理店

UMEDA

御料理 梅田

- [ ] Address : Aioi Insurance Ninety Yokohama Building 2F , 4-52, Bentendori, Naka-ku, Yokohama-shi, Kanagawa
- [ ] Design : ozi design works inc. / Ryosuke Hashimoto
- [ ] 住所 ： 神奈川県横浜市中区弁天通4-52 あいおい損保・ナインティー横浜ビル2F
- [ ] 設計 ： オジデザインワークス㈲ / 橋本 亮介

A Japanese restaurant that fuses tradition and innovation

The owner of this establishment adopted a style that could express modernity whilst safeguarding the food culture he learned in Kyoto. Its location of Yokohama's Bashamichi, where tradition and progress harmoniously coexist, is in keeping with this approach, as is the series of innovative ideas that distinguish the interior. Like a hodgepodge of the history that the owner and diners have built together, materials that age beautifully, like tin tiles and the leather used for the counter are a crucial design point here.

伝統と革新へのチャレンジ精神を象徴する和食店の設え

京都で身につけた和食の文化を守りつつ、柔軟な発想で進歩していくというスタイルを持つ店主。このスタイルとリンクする横浜馬車道という伝統と進化が共存する地で、ベースを押さえながらも既成概念に囚われないデザインで、店主の姿勢を表現している。客と店主が築く歴史を刻むかのように、オリジナルの錫のタイルや革のカウンターという、時を経て徐々に良さが滲み出る素材使いが印象的。

1

1 The facade	1 ファサード
2 The metal tiles on the floor and mosaic tiles on the pillars evoke a refined look	2 床の金属タイルとモザイクタイル貼りの柱が高級感を創出

4

3 The table seating as seen from the passageway

4 The counter seating designed to harmonize with lacquer ware

3 通路よりテーブル席を見る

4 漆器との調和が美しいカウンター席

UMEDA

Opening Hours:Lunch 11:30~14:00 Dinner17:30~22:00 Holidays:Sunday and National
Holiday Tel:045-651-9184 Customer:30s-50s men and women Floor Space:72.10㎡
Seats:29(included counter 5) Opened:14/11/2005 Operated by:Kensuke Umeda
Design:ozi design works inc. Contractor:soar-zoken Cooperator:Gallery Ukou
Photographs:Kanta Ushio

御料理 梅田

営業時間:ランチ11:30～14:00 ディナー17:30～22:00 定休日:日・祝 Tel:045-651-9184 来
客者層:30代～50代の男女 店舗面積:72.10㎡ 席数:29席（内カウンター5席） 開店日:2005年
11月14日 経営:梅田 健介 設計:オジデザインワークス㈲ 施工:㈱ソアー造研 協力:ギャラリー
卯甲 撮影:牛尾 幹太

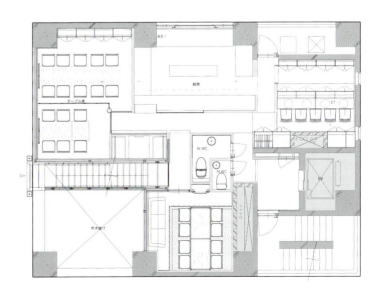

Yurari Kirari

和食レストラン ゆらり・きらり

☐ Address ：SHIESPA 1F , 1-28-1 Shoto, Shibuya-ku, Tokyo
☐ Design ：SPOIL ASSOCIATES INC. / Shu Yamashita

☐ 住所 ：東京都渋谷区松濤1-28-1 SHIESPA 1 F
☐ 設計 ：スポイル・アソシエイツ㈱ / 山下 秀

A space that incorporates natural elements to heal mind and body

Bearing in mind the fact that it is attached to a private bathhouse, this Japanese restaurant was designed to serve as healing space catering to a broad range of clientele. Rooted in a Japanese aesthetic, the interior uses natural materials to evoke a sense of warmth as well as a soothing, clean look, making it somewhere to enjoy food and conversation at a leisurely pace. A terrace area removed from the main body of the space features plants and sunlight, as well as a bar and a bank of relaxation chairs. This is an urban oasis with a menu and ambience that are beneficial for body and soul.

心身を癒す自然の要素を取り込んだ食空間

温浴施設の一角である事から、幅広い客層に対応できる「癒しの空間」という位置づけの和食店。和を基調に温かみある天然素材を用いて「優しさと清潔感」を出し、ゆったりと食事や会話を楽しめる場となっている。別室には、植栽や太陽光等の自然要素を取り入れたテラスエリアがあり、バーやリラクゼーションチェアでも寛げる。身体に良い食と空間に安らぐ都会のオアシスとなった。

1

1　The counter seating area　　1　カウンター席
2　A party room　　2　パーティールーム

3　The bar seating beside
　　the relaxation corner
4　The relaxation corner as viewed from
　　the outdoor terrace

3　リラクゼーションコーナー横の
　　バーカウンター席
4　屋外テラス席よりリラクゼーション
　　コーナーを見る

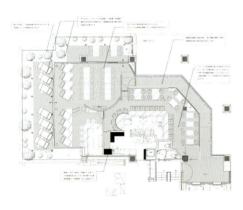

Yurari Kirari

Opening Hours:11:00~9:00 Holidays:Irregular Tel:03-3477-2100 Customer:Over 20s
Females Floor Space:180.19㎡ Seats:Restaurant 46(counter12, tables34) Multipurpose
salon seats24(indoor seats16, terrace8) relaxation corner 21(bar6, indoor seats 8, ter-
race7) Opened:1/2006 Operated by:UNIMAT FUTURE Design:SPOIL ASSOCIATES
INC. Contractor:Forme Co., Ltd. Cooperator:TAISEI CORPORATION, AIDEC Co.,Ltd,
USHIOSPAX, Inc. Photographs:Nacása & Partners inc.

和食レストラン ゆらり・きらり

営業時間:11:00～翌9:00 定休日:不定休 Tel:03-3477-2100 来客者層:20代以上の女性客
店舗面積:180.19㎡ 席数:レストランスペース46席(カウンター12席、テーブル34席)多目的サロ
ン24席(室内16席、テラス8席)リラクゼーションコーナー21席(バー6席、室内8席、テラス7席)
開店日:2006年1月 経営:㈱ユニマットフューチャー 設計:スポイル・アソシエイツ㈱ 施工:㈱フォ
ルム 協力:大成建設㈱ アイデック㈱ ウシオスペックス 撮影:Nacása & Partners inc.

003 | JAPANESE
日本料理

Edomae-Style sushi
江戸前寿司

JUN

鮨処 順 丸の内店

☐ Address：Mitsubishi Shoji BuildingB1F, 2-3-1, Marunouchi, Chiyoda-ku, Tokyo
☐ Design ：KENGO KUMA & ASSOCIATES / Kengo Kuma

☐ 住所 ：東京都千代田区丸の内2-3-1 三菱商事ビルB1F
☐ 設計 ：㈱隈研吾建築都市設計事務所 / 隈 研吾

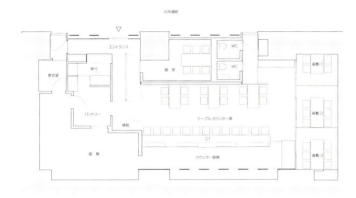

A presentation in the lightness of a basement interior by a stone pottery artist

This restaurant carries on the spirit of traditional Edomae sushi, offering seasonal ingredients and flavors without any thought towards the labor involved. Built as a collaboration with stone pottery artist Shinichi Mogi, the interior has been designed using Shirakawa stone from Fukushima prefecture that has had its color altered using firing temperatures and time. The entrance and area behind the counter inside feature fired pieces hanging from flat bars, while the "hole" wall surface of the basement area is presented with light stones. The suspended baked stones stand out like flower petals, and lend a sense of light and flowing wind to the interior of the restaurant.

石の陶芸家と目指した地下空間の軽さの表現

旬の素材と味に手間を惜しまず、伝統ある江戸前寿司の真髄を伝える店。石の陶芸家茂木真一氏とのコラボレーションにより、焼成の温度と時間で色に変化をつけた福島県産白河石をデザインした。エントランスと店内カウンターバックには焼成体をフラットバーで吊り下げ、地下空間に「孔」の壁面を軽い石で表現。焼成石を吊る事で軽やかな花びらの様に見立て、店内を光と風が吹き抜ける様を表している。

1

1 Lightness is expressed through the rhythmical arrangement of the baked stones 1 石の焼成体をリズミカルに配置する事で軽やかさを表現

2 The contrast between the darkness of the unfired stone of the floor and the fired stone of the walls is charming

3 The un-seamed taiko-style washi paper light screen is warm

4 Private seating separated by washi paper partitions

2 床の焼成前の石の黒目と壁の焼成体のコントラストが魅力

3 繋ぎ目のない和紙太鼓貼りの光のスクリーンが温か

4 和紙貼りのパーテーションで仕切る個室

JUN

Opening Hours:Weekday 11:30~14:00 17:00~22:00(L.O.21:30) Saturday and Sunday and National Holiday 11:30~21:00(L.O.20:30) Holidays:None Tel:03-6212-8800 Customer:Women in the afternoons, Those aged 20 to 60 or families at night Floor Space:152.2㎡ Seats:47(counter13, tables12, kotatsu set in the floor style16, private room private room table6) Opened:25/4/2006 Operated by:JUN-SUSHI.Co.,Ltd. Design:KENGO KUMA & ASSOCIATES Contractor:NOMURA Co.,Ltd. Cooperator:Shinichi Mogi Photographs:JPA Shooting

鮨処 順 丸の内店

営業時間:平日11:30~14:00 17:00~22:00（L.O.21:30）土・日・祝11:30~21:00(L.O.20:30) 定休日:無休 Tel:03-6212-8800 来客者層:昼は女性、夜は20代〜60代又はその家族 店舗面積:152.2㎡ 席数:47席（カウンター13席、テーブル12席、座敷掘り炬燵式16席、個室テーブル6席） 開店日:2006年4月25日 経営:㈲順寿司 設計:㈱隈研吾建築都市設計事務所 施工:㈱乃村工藝社 協力:茂木 真一 撮影:JPAシューティング

YUZUYA ISSHINKYO

柚子屋 一心居

☐ Address：Tokai Annex Building 1F, 3-16-8, Akasaka, Minato-ku, Tokyo
☐ Design：FIRST KIWA PLANNING Co., Ltd. / Hirokazu Sakamaki

☐ 住所：東京都港区赤坂3-16-8 東海アネックスビル1F
☐ 設計：ファースト キワ・プランニング㈱ / 坂槇 洋和

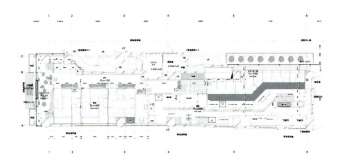

1

Japanese-style space inspired by Kyoto style in the Akasaka area

This Kyoto-style restaurant makes plentiful use of vegetables from the Kyoto area. An oasis of calm in the bustling business district of Akasaka, it fuses the beauty of traditional Japanese style with modern elements. The theme, "A bamboo grove in the middle of the city," captures the notion of contrasts, and the main seating area and raised dining area are centered around the kitchen. An alley that links two separate zones is lined with thick bamboo that extends as far as the ceiling, and is a dynamic expression if typical Kyoto style. As an annex to the Kyoto Yuzuya Japanese-style inn, it has a particularly refined atmosphere.

京の風情漂う赤坂一ツ木通り沿いの和空間

京野菜をふんだんに使った京料理の店。繁華街にありながらも静けさが漂い、伝統の和の美しさと現代的な要素が同居する。この相反するコンセプトを共存させるため、「都会の中の竹林」をテーマに、厨房を中心に座席と小上がり席を配置。二つの空間を結ぶ路地は天井に届く孟宗竹で覆い、京都に見る竹垣をダイナミックに表現している。京都柚子屋旅館別館としての位置づけを呈し、凛とした空気が包む空間。

1 The entrance, with outer wall shrouded in thick bamboo that echoes the feature inside
2 The counter seating area in back of the space where Kyoto-style stone brazier holders are displayed in a row

1 外壁を孟宗竹で覆いつくし内部との連帯を表現した入口
2 おくどさんが並ぶ店内奥のカウンター席

3　A passageway designed to looked like that of an old Kyoto-style house
4　A tatami mat room located just of the corridor

3　京町家の鰻の寝床のような路地
4　通路横にある座敷を見る

4

YUZUYA ISSHINKYO

Opening Hours:11:30~15:00(L.O.14:00)18:00~23:00(L.O.22:00) Sunday and National Holiday17:00~21:00(L.O.) Holidays:None Tel:03-5545-6314 Customer:30s-40s Those working in the area welcomed, as well as middle-aged and older couples living nearby Family Floor Space:135㎡ Seats:33(counter15, parlors for4, for12, for 2) Opened:7/2005 Operated by:KIWA CORPORATION Co.,Ltd. Design:FIRST KIWA PLANNING Co., Ltd. Contractor:CREATIVE M Co.,LTD. Photographs:JPA Shooting

柚子屋 一心居

営業時間:11:30~15:00（L.O.14:00）18:00~23:00（L.O.22:00）日・祝17:00~21:00（L.O.）定休日:無休Tel:03-5545-6314 来客者層:30代~40代 近隣在勤者接待利用,近隣在住中高年夫婦,ファミリー 店舗面積:135㎡ 席数:33席（カウンター15席，座敷4席／6席×2／2席）開店日:2005年7月 経営:際コーポレーション㈱ 設計:ファーストキワ・プランニング㈱ 施工:㈱クリエイティブ エム 撮影:JPAシューティング

Kyotaru

京樽総本店

☐ Address：Glan Sweet Nihonbashi Ningyocho1F, 2-7-5, Nihonbashi Ningyocho, Chuo-ku, Tokyo

☐ Design ：NOMURA Co., Ltd. / Yuji Hirata, Toshihito Kato

☐ 住所 ：東京都中央区日本橋人形町2-7-5 グランスイート日本橋人形町1F

☐ 設計 ：㈱乃村工藝社 / 平田 裕二・加藤 利仁

The history and modernism of a famous restaurant that enchants guests with its tea room design

With a proud history spanning over 70 years, Kyotaru Sou Honten is known as a favorite dining spot of noted individuals from many different fields. Using the theme "a modern tea room", something that could only be possible today, the interior has been embellished with elements such as thin and delicate lattice and plaster that shines with an elegant radiance. After ducking through the entrance, which still features its old appearance, guests travel down a lane until coming upon the quiet table seating on their right. Each of the 3 private rooms leading of the footpath has a different decorative alcove, making them into spaces that will impress visitors with their warmth and high class design.

**数寄屋デザインが魅せる
名店の歴史とモダニズム**

各界著名人に愛され、70年以上もの歴史を誇る『京樽総本店』。現代こそ可能な「モダンな数奇屋」をテーマに、薄く繊細な「格子」や品のある輝きを放った「左官」等、随所にその要素を散りばめている。かつての面影を残す玄関を潜り、路地を抜けた左手は落ち着いたテーブル席。踏込みから導かれる3つの個室はそれぞれ異なった床の間を持ち、格式高い設えが出迎える温かみある空間となった。

1

1　The hospitable low entrance has remained unchanged since the business was established　　1　創業時よりある「蹲」を取り入れた風情あるエントランス

2　A peek at the serene miniature garden
3　The "Sakura" table seating
4　The "Fuji" private room
5　The "Ayame" private room

2　心和ませる箱庭をのぞむ
3　テーブル席「桜」
4　個室「藤」
5　個室「菖蒲」

4

KYOTARU

Opening Hours:11:00~15:00 17:00~22:00(L.O.21:00) Take
Out 10:00~20:00 Holidays:None Tel:03-3666-5445
Customer:The class of old and middle age, business dinner
Floor Space:297.69㎡ Seats:40(tables 22, parlor18)
Renewal:11/7/2005 Operated by:Kyotaru Co., Ltd.
Design:NOMURA Co., Ltd. Contractor:NOMURA Co., Ltd.
Cooperator:IDEAL Co., Ltd. Photographs:JPA Shooting

京樽総本店

営業時間:11:00~15:00 17:00~22:00(L.O.21:00)テイクアウ
ト10:00~20:00 定休日:無休 Tel:03-3666-5445 来客者層:中
高年層、接待 店舗面積:297.69㎡ 席数:40席(テーブル22席、
座敷18席) 改装日:2005年7月11日 経営:㈱京樽 設計:㈱乃
村工藝社 施工:㈱乃村工藝社 撮影:JPAシューティング

JISHU
時習

☐ Address ：3-11-7, Higashi-ikebukuro, Toshima-ku, Tokyo
☐ Design ：STUDIO NAGARE Co., Ltd. / Akira Yokoi

☐ 住所 ：東京都豊島区東池袋3-11-7
☐ 設計 ：㈱スタジオナガレ / 横井 晃

An modeled interior with modern-day traditional forms

The concept at work here is "representation". The interior space has been made using conventional Japanese construction methods with fan lights, tatami, paper sliding doors and lattice in a way that almost makes it into a perfect representation of classic tradition and etiquette. However, in order to calmly blend such an environment with the sensibilities of the present, traditional forms from modern culture have been sublimated as well. Take for instance the private room modeled after a barrel, or the sliding door back bar that can be seen over the fan lights. While these Japanese materials have arranged in a stimulating manner, the interior has been designed so that they work together in perfect harmony.

空間に象った現代版の伝統様式

コンセプトは「象（katadori）」。日本建築の伝統的な欄間や畳、障子格子を使い、伝統や作法を刻印するかのように室内空間を象る。そして、現代に溶け込んで感覚的に落ち着くよう、現代文化に昇華させた伝統様式だ。樽をイメージした個室。欄間越しから見える障子のバックバー。和の素材一つ一つを刺激的に配置しつつも、それらが全て滑らかに同調するように空間を構成している。

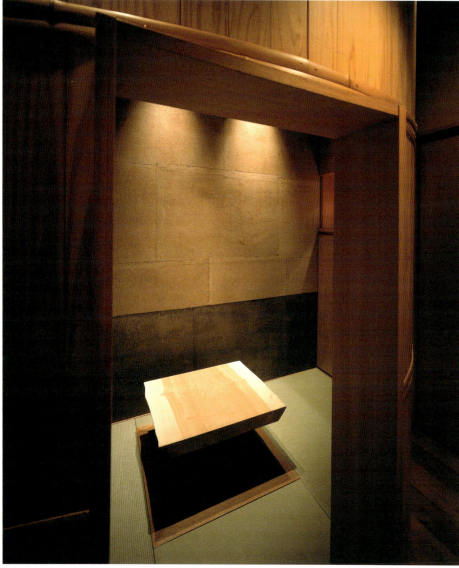

1　The barrel-like private room
2　Counter seating seen over the fan lights

1　樽のような個室
2　欄間越しに見るカウンター席

1

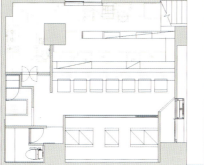

JISHU

Opening Hours:Lunch11:30~14:30 Dinner17:30~22:00 Holidays:Saturday and Sunday and National Holiday Tel:03-3987-7630 Customer:Office worker Floor Space:50㎡ Seats:19(counter7, parlor10, private room2) Opened:12/2005 Operated by:Hironobu Sugita Design:STUDIO NAGARE Co., Ltd. Contractor:Hasegawa Kenko Inc. Cooperator:Tanabe carpenter Photographs:Nacása & Partners inc.

時習

営業時間:ランチ11:30～14:30 ディナー17:30～22:00 定休日:土・日・祝 Tel:03-3987-7630 来客者層:サラリーマン 店舗面積:50㎡ 席数:19席（カウンター7席、座敷10席、個室2席） 開店日:2005年12月 経営:杉田 博宣 設計:㈱スタジオナガレ 施工:有長谷川建工 協力:有田辺建具 撮影:Nacása & Partners inc.

nagomidokoro haretoke

和処 晴と褻

☐ Address ：Kyobashi AK Building B1F , 3-3-14, Kyobashi, Chuo-ku, Tokyo
☐ Design ：Takato Tamagami Architectural Design / Takato Tamagami

☐ 住所 ：東京都中央区京橋3-3-14 京橋AKビルB1F
☐ 設計 ：タカト タマガミデザイン / 玉上 貴人

The embodiment of the extraordinary
through the goodness of natural materials

The concept of Haretoke is the extraordinary and the ordinary. In order to live up to the meaning of its name as a place of harmony, all efforts have made here to create a splendid presentation that is free of any sense of tension. Features of the interior such as the Japanese cypress counter tops, Japanese washi paper, and earthen walls blend together to show the high quality and warmth of natural materials. Perhaps the defining point of this restaurant is the small door of the entrance, which has the same idea behind it as the door of a tea ceremony room in that social status and authority are removed when guests pass through so that all can enjoy a comfortable time as equals.

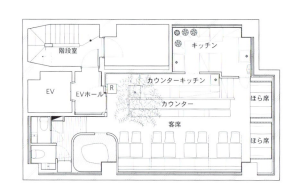

自然素材の良さが肩のこらない非日常を具現

「非日常と日常」がコンセプト。あくまで和処（なごみどころ）という事を前提に、華美な演出や緊張感を出さぬように工夫。檜のカウンターや和紙、土壁等を使用して素材の高級感を溶け込ませ、自然素材の温もりを感じる空間としている。入口の躙り口は茶室の考え方そのままに、地位や権力など全てを取り払い、スペースを共有する者全て平等に心地良い時を、との店の思いがこもったこだわりポイント。

1

1　The entrance features nicely textured yakisugi cypress
2　The single-board counter seating is conspicuous for the quality its Japanese cypress

1　焼き杉の風合いが良いエントランス
2　素材の良さが際立つ檜の一枚板カウンター席

3 Table seating placed in shadow by light shining through creased walls of hung Japanese paper

4 Cavern seating that features sound-absorbent urethane rubber padding all the way to the ceiling

5 A private room features large straw mixed with diatomaceous clay for an artless look

3 シワを出した和紙貼りの壁に照明で
　　陰影をつけたテーブル席

4 ウレタンラバーで天井まで覆い
　　吸音作用も実現したほら席

5 大きな藁を珪藻土に混ぜ、素朴感を
　　出した個室

nagomidokoro haretoke

Opening Hours:Weekday11:30~24:00 Holidays:Saturday and Sunday and National Holiday Tel:03-3517-8008 Customer:30s-40s men and women Floor Space:71.28㎡ Seats:40(1private room for 6, 2 half-private-room for 4, counter 8-11, tables 16-18) Opened:4/8/2005 Operated by:oneten.inc Design:Takato Tamagami Architectural Design Contractor:kinari Photographs:Tomoki Hayakawa

和処 晴と藝

営業時間:月～金11:30～24:00　定休日:土・日・祝　Tel:03-3517-8008　来客者層:30代～40代　男女　店舗面積:71.28㎡　席数:約40席（個室6×1室、半個室4×2室、カウンター8～11席、テーブル16～18席）開店日:2005年8月4日　経営:㈲ワンテン　設計:タカト タマガミデザイン　施工:キナリ　撮影:早川 友紀

008	JAPANESE 日本料理店

Conger eel Cuisine,
Japanese Cuisine,
Warmed Sake
あなご料理、和食、燗酒

Hakarime

あなご燗酒 はかりめ

- ☐ Address：Cheers Ginza6F, 5-9-5, Ginza, Chuo-ku, Tokyo
- ☐ Design ：bis at'tic inc. / Masahiro Shiomi

- ☐ 住所　：東京都中央区銀座5-9-5 チアーズ銀座6F
- ☐ 設計　：㈱ビス・アティック / 塩見 政広

**A simple Japanese-style interior with good material sense that fits
the business type and name**

This specialist shop presents various ways of eating anago conger eel. Upon opening the lattice door and entering the establishment, it becomes apparent the long central hallway running the length of the interior is meant to divide the space into two separate well-balanced scenes of action and stillness. The scene of stillness is made up of a succession of Japanese lattice screens that invite one's eyes to gaze deeper into the heart of the restaurant. On the other hand the scene of activity conveys the scents and noise of the kitchen over a pure horse chestnut counter. Built entirely of natural materials of a similar color such as wood and Japanese washi paper, the final result is a mature space that is fashionably orthodox.

業態と店名に合わせたシンプルかつ素材感のある和空間

穴子の種々の食べ方を提案する専門店。格子戸を開け店内へ進むと、一本の長い廊下を中心に「静と動」の二つの景色がバランス良く空間を仕切る。静の景色は、視点を奥へと誘い空間の奥行きをより深める連続した和格子のスクリーンで構成。もう一方は、栃無垢のカウンター越しに音や香りを伝える動の景色だ。全体を木や和紙等同系色の自然素材が包む、正統派の粋な大人の空間に仕上った。

1

1　The entrance as seen from the elevator hall
2　The counter can be seen from near the entrance

1　エレベーターホールからエントランスを見る
2　入口近くからカウンターを見る

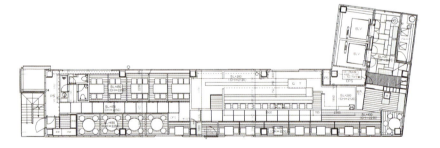

3　One of the long table private rooms as seen from the corridor

3　廊下から長卓個室を見る

4　A round table private room

4　円卓個室

Hakarime

Opening Hours:Lunch 12:00~14:30 Dinner Weekday17:30~23:30 Saturday 17:00~23:30 Sunday and National Holiday17:00~23:00 Holidays:Closed for the New Year Holiday Tel:03-6253-7070 Customer:30s-60s men and women Floor Space:171㎡ Seats:72(counter12, 18private rooms for 60) Opened:15/3/2005 Operated by:MARUYAMA SHOUJI Design:bis at'tic inc. Contractor:NISSHO INTER LIFE Co., Ltd. Cooperator:Display:BLUE PLANTS / Manabu Hirano Photographs:SHIN PHOTOWORK Inc. / Shinji Miyamoto

あなご燗酒 はかりめ

営業時間：ランチ12:00~14:30 ディナー月~金17:30~23:30 土17:00~23:30 日・祝17:00~23:00 定休日：年末年始 Tel:03-6253-7070 来客者層：30代~60代 男女 店舗面積：171㎡ 席数：72席（カウンター12席、個室18室／60席） 開店日：2005年3月15日 経営：丸山商事㈱ 設計：㈱ビス・アティック 施工：㈱日商インターライフ 協力：ディスプレイ：ブループランツ / 平野 学 撮影：㈲シンフォトワーク / 宮本 真治

Suzunari

スズナリ

☐ Address ：Araki-cho7, Shinjuku-ku, Tokyo
☐ Design ：STUDIO NAGARE Co., Ltd. / Takahiro Yokoi
☐ 住所 ：東京都新宿区荒木町7
☐ 設計 ：㈱スタジオナガレ / 横井 貴広

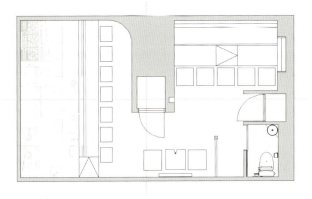

A rediscovery of Japanese culture through the use of the inherent flavors of materials

This 10 tsubo establishment invites guests to come in and relax with its large frontage on the corner of an old-school dining strip. The design concept is "a simple touch". The decision to go with a simple interior started with the viewpoint that a stripped-down interior would actually clarify a guest's senses, while the touch of wood would allow them to enjoy themselves heartily. Traditional materials such as the unfinished wood of the pre-existing pillars and the plaster used in the walls make for a coziness that possesses a harmonious balance between the old and the new.

素材の持ち味を生かす日本の文化を再認識

10坪程度で営む店が古くより連なる飲食店街の一角で、利用者が安心して入れるよう間口を大きく取った。そのデザインコンセプトは「Simple Touch」。削ぎ落とされた空間こそ、人間の五感は研ぎ澄まされ、木に触れる感覚を心から楽しむことができるという観点から、シンプルな空間構成に。既存の柱に無垢材、左官壁等の伝統的素材を使用し、新旧の調和が取れた、居心地の良さを生み出した。

1

1　The entrance and its impressive plaster walls　　1　左官壁が印象的なエントランス

3

2 The single plank unfinished wood counter

3 The single plank set against the wall is quite impressive

2 無垢材の一枚板のカウンター

3 壁に立てかけられた一枚板が印象的

Suzunari

Opening Hours:18:00~24:00 Holidays:Sunday and National Holiday Tel:03-3530-1178
Customer:Office worker, women, couples Floor Space:24.5㎡ Seats:19(counter7, table12)
Opened:16/12/2005 Operated by:Akihiko Murata Design:STUDIO NAGARE Co., Ltd.
Contractor:Hasegawa Kenko Inc. Photographs:Nacása & Partners inc.

Suzunari

営業時間:18:00～24:00　定休日:日・祝 Tel:03-3530-1178 来客者層:サラリーマン, 女性, カップル
店舗面積:24.5㎡ 席数:19席（カウンター7席, テーブル12席）開店日:2005年12月16日　経営:村田
明彦 設計:㈱スタジオナガレ 施工:㈲長谷川建工 撮影:Nacása & Partners inc.

KINNOKANI

金の蟹

☐ Address : Shiroyama Trust Tower 2F, 4-3-1, Toranomon, Minato-ku, Tokyo
☐ Design : Merchandising Organization Co., Ltd. / Tomokazu Nagao, Sayuri Somemiya

☐ 住所 : 東京都港区虎ノ門4-3-1 城山トラストタワー2F
☐ 設計 : ㈱マーチャンダイジング・オーガニゼーション / 永尾 友和・染宮 小百合

A refined Japanese space that makes good use of the expression of unfinished wood

The design theme of Kinnokani is that of a Japanese reception hall. Much thought has been put into making this a space where guests can feel the heartfelt hospitality found throughout Japanese culture. Japanese-style tables that feature the striking cleanliness of unfinished wood as a keynote have been placed strategically so as to give rise to a modern air. The kitchen area is completely open, furthering enhancing the presence of the restaurant by allowing guests to watch chefs preparing of crab dishes.

白木の表情を生かした雅びな和空間

デザインテーマは"迎賓館"。日本の文化を随所に感じる空間で心のこもったおもてなしを、との想いが込められた。清潔感溢れる白木を基調とし、モダンな空気を生む和のディテールを随所に設けた。キッチンスペースは限りなくオープンにし、蟹をさばく料理人の姿を見せる事で臨場感を演出する。

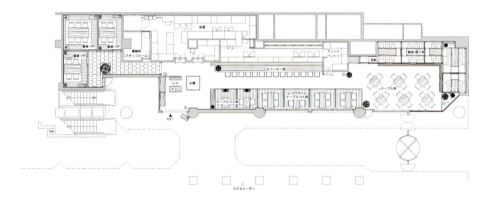

1

1 A view of the facade
2 A view of the hall

1 ファサードを見る
2 ホールを見る

3 Looking towards to the counter seating from the hall
4 A view of the landscaped garden from a private room

3 ホールからカウンター席方面を見る
4 個室から造園を見る

KINNOKANI

Opening Hours:11:30~22:30 Holidays:Saturday and National Holiday Tel:03-5425-1101 Customer:businessman Floor Space:297.3㎡ Seats:100 Opened:7/11/2005 Operated by:KANI YA HONKE Design:Merchandising Organization Co., Ltd. Contractor: MT FACILITY SERVICE Co., Ltd. Cooperator:Outer wall picture production Junko Suzuki Photographs:Kaoru Kitahara

金の蟹

営業時間:11:30~22:30 定休日:日・祝 Tel:03-5425-1101 来客者層:ビジネスマン 店舗面積:297.3㎡ 席数:100席 開店日:2005年11月7日 経営:㈱かに家本家 設計:㈱マーチャンダイジング・オーガニゼーション 施工:MTファシリティサービス㈱ 協力:外壁絵画制作 鈴木 淳子 撮影:北原 薫

SHIMBASHI-HATSUFUJI

しんばし初藤

☐ Address ：New Shimbashi Building 2F , 2-16-11 , Shimbashi, Minato-ku, Tokyo
☐ Design ：Kamiya Design Inc. / Toshinori Kamiya , Aya Otaki

☐ 住所 ：東京都港区新橋2-16-11 ニュー新橋ビル2F
☐ 設計 ：㈱神谷デザイン事務所 / 神谷 利徳・大瀧 綾

Clever use of bamboo for a light-hearted Japanese presentation

This marks the first complete renovation in twenty years for Shimbashi Hatsufuji, which opened during the period of postwar recovery in 1949 as a food cart in front of Shimbashi Station. Starting with its two story facade on the building in front the station, the presentation here is one of a casual, bright, and healthy image of Japan realized through the texture of bamboo and wood on all surfaces. Bamboo partition, parts of which have been hollowed out and used as display space for spirits, smartly divide up the large table area. The bamboo seen through the lattice of receives its moisture from the old building.

竹を巧みに利用した軽やかな和の演出

戦後復興期の昭和23年、新橋駅前で屋台から始まった『しんばし初藤』が20年ぶりの全面改装。新橋駅前に建つビル2階のファサードより、竹や木の質感を全面に打ち出してカジュアルで明るい健康的な和のイメージを表現。竹のパーティションは一部をくりぬき酒のディスプレイに利用され、大テーブルの空間を程よく区切る。共用部から見える格子越しの竹のディスプレイは、古くから建つビルに潤いを与える。

1

2

1 The entrance
2 The thick moso bamboo partitions also serve as displays for bottles
3 The large table seating

1 エントランス
2 ボトルディスプレイも兼ねた孟宗竹のパーティション
3 大テーブル席

5

4 Indian-ink drawing
5 Seating for incognito visits

4 テーブル席越しに書を見る
5 お忍び席

SHIMBASHI-HATSUFUJI

Opening Hours:Weekday 11:00~14:00 16:00~22:00(L.O.)Friday11:00~14:00 16:00~22:30(L.O.)Saturday and National Holiday 11:00~21:30(L.O.) Holidays:Sunday Tel:03-3580-2856 Customer:35s-50s Floor Space:178.2㎡ Seats:74(counter 14, table 32, 3private rooms for 28) Renewal:13/9/2005 Operated by:NIHON SHOKUHIN SHOJI Co.,Ltd. Design:Kamiya Design Inc. Contractor:SHIBA-SANGYOU INC. Cooperator:Illumination:KOIZU-MI LIGHTING TECHNOLOGY CORP, Plasterer:HaNaSaKa-DaN Special order illumination:WATTS Special order bamboo:Shizen-no-Kaze Photographs:Masahiro Ishibashi

しんばし初藤

営業時間:平日11:00~14:00 16:00~22:00(L.O.)金11:00~14:00 16:00~22:30(L.O.)土・祝11:00~21:30(L.O.) 定休日:日曜 Tel:03-3580-2856 来客者層:35~50代 店舗面積:178.2㎡ 席数:74席(カウンター14席、テーブル32席、個室3部屋/28席)改装日:2005年9月13日 経営:日本食品商事(株) 設計:(株)神谷デザイン事務 施工:芝産業(株) 協力:照明:コイズミ照明(株) 左官:花咲か団 特注照明:(株)ワッツ 特注竹:自然の風 撮影:石橋 マサヒロ

chacha yufu-dachi

茶茶白雨 -ゆふだち-

☐ Address ： Kawano Building 6F, 3-26-18, Shinjuku, Shinjuku-ku, Tokyo
☐ Design ： Moon Balance,Inc. / Hisanobu Tsujimura

☐ 住所 ： 東京都新宿区新宿3-26-18 カワノビル6F
☐ 設計 ： 辻村久信デザイン事務所＋㈱ムーンバランス / 辻村 久信

1

The Japanese sense of beauty harvested for an in-building eatery

Tucked away on the sixth floor of the East Exit building of Shinjuku Station, this restaurant serves mainly Kyoto-style dishes using all the traditional ingredients. Despite being located inside the totally man-made environment of a building, the sense of beauty the Japanese have developed from centuries of living in harmony with nature has been incorporated to give the interior an artificial sense of the earthiness. In a touch of encompassing abstractness, the low-ceiling and limited dining space has been designed to accentuate the relationship of interior and exterior, so that the interior of the restaurant feels like the outdoors, while the exterior appears to be indoors.

ビルインの店舗に取り入れた
日本人の美意識

JR新宿駅東口側のビル6階に位置し、京都の食材をふんだんに使用した京都おばんざいを中心に提供する店舗。自然もない完全に囲われたビルインの空間に、自然と共存するような暮らし方をしてきた日本人の美意識を取り入れ、仮想の自然を内部空間に創っている。包容力のある抽象性とともに、天井の低い限られた空間を内外に分けて、内は外を外は内を景色とする事で、互いの関係性をデザインしている。

1　The lattice door of the inviting entrance softly conveys the presence and light of the outside world

1　風情溢れる入口の格子戸が外の気配と
　　光を柔らかく伝える

chacha yufu-dachi

Opening Hours:17:00~1:00 Holidays:None Tel:03-5368-6302 Customer:Late20s-30s
Floor Space:331.84㎡ Seats:136 Opened:11/11/2005 Operated by:Jellyfish.Co,.ltd.
Design:Moon Balance,Inc. Contractor:CIRCUS Photographs:JPA Shooting

茶茶白雨 -ゆふだち-

営業時間:17:00～翌1:00 定休日:無休 Tel:03-5368-6302 来客者層:20代後半～30代 店舗
面積:331.84㎡ 席数:136席 開店日:2005年11月11日 経営:Jellyfish.㈱ 設計:辻村久信デザ
イン事務所＋㈱ムーンバランス 施工:㈱サーカス 撮影:JPAシューティング

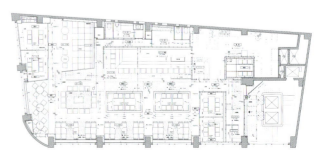

2 A view of the counter and its modern ambience
3 Table seating soothes the heart with abstracted plant objet d'art and green bamboo
4 Elevated seating in the heart of the interior

2 モダンな雰囲気のカウンターを見る
3 植物を抽象化した壁のオブジェと青竹に心和むテーブル席
4 店内奥の小上がり席

4

Japanese Dining Kiryu

ジャパニーズダイニング 樹龍

☐ Address：Roger Aoyama 1F, 1-4-5, Kita-Aoyama, Minato-ku, Tokyo
☐ Produce：Daiko Holdings Corporation / Hironori Satoh
☐ Design：SoLC Architects / Tatsuya Ogawa

☐ 住所　：東京都港区北青山1-4-5 ロジェ青山1F
☐ プロデュース　：ダイコーホールディングス㈱ / 佐藤 裕憲
☐ 設計　：SoLC建築設計事務所 / 小川 達也

A fog screen interface with the city

The entrance of this restaurant facing Route 246 features as its facade a fog screen that is 8.7 meters tall by 5.7 meters tall. The meter deep space between the double screens has been filled with mist so that the only the pale light escapes to the outside. Meanwhile, the inner screen serves as a backdrop for the projection of various images. The interior of the restaurant has been finished as a light and fantastic scene contrary to the image of materials by a curved surface of curved drapes containing louvers made of hard heavy stone and metal mesh.

都市とのインターフェイスとなるフォグスクリーン

246通り沿いに面するファサードに高さ8.7×幅5.7mのフォグスクリーンを設置。奥行1mのダブルスキン内に霧を充満させ、外部へは淡い光を放ち、内部へは様々な映像を映すスクリーンとして機能する。内装は、硬く重い石による有機的な形状のルーバーやメタルメッシュの曲線のドレープ加工による曲面により、素材の持つイメージと相反する軽やかで幻想的なシーンに仕上っている。

1

1　The exterior. The fog screen glows with the light it disperses
2　Organically-shaped stone louvers enclose the first floor hall

1　外観　霧に照明が拡散して光るフォグスクリーン
2　有機的な形状の石ルーバーが囲う1階ホール

3　The second floor hall glitters with soft metal mesh drapes

4　Linear metal mesh stairs lit by LED lighting

5　Second floor private seating with imagery based off gold and lacquer (At the center is a gold leaf panel)

3　柔らかなドレープ状のメタルメッシュが輝く2階ホール

4　LED照明をあてた直線的メタルメッシュがかかる階段

5　金と漆をイメージした2階個室（中央は金箔パネル）

4

5

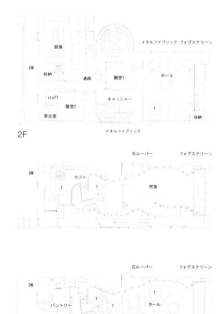

2F

1F

Japanese Dining Kiryu

Opening Hours:Weekday 11:30~15:00 17:00~23:00 Saturday and Sunday and National Holiday11:30~16:00 17:00~21:00 Holidays:Every third Sunday Tel:03-5785-9361 Customer:30s-40s Floor Space:265.55 ㎡ Seats:56 Opened:2/9/2005 Operated by:D's creation, Ltd. Produce:Daiko Holdings Corporation Design:SoLC Architects Contractor:K's planning Co., Ltd. + Tomatsu Co.,Ltd Photographs:Etsu Moriyama

ジャパニーズダイニング 樹龍

営業時間:平日11:30～15:00 17:00～23:00土・日・祝11:30～16:00 17:00～21:00 定休日:第3日曜 Tel:03-5785-9361 来客者層:30～40代 店鋪面積:265.55㎡ 席数:56席 開店日:2005年9月2日 経営:㈱D's Creation プロデュース:ダイコーホールディングス㈱ 設計:SoLC建築設計事務所 施工:㈲ケイズプランニング+㈱戸松 撮影:森山 越

restaurant morimoto XEX

レストランモリモト ゼックス

☐ Address ：I.K.N Roppongi Building, 7-21-19, Roppongi, Minato-ku, Tokyo
☐ Design ：spin off co., ltd. / Ichiro Shiomi , Etsuko Yamamoto

☐ 住所 ：東京都港区六本木7-21-19 I.K.N六本木ビル
☐ 設計 ：スピン・オフ / 塩見 一郎・山本 英津子

A restaurant full of the excitement and radiance of a night at the theater

This is the restaurant opened by Masaharu Morimoto, who gained fame as the third Iron Chef Japanese on the television program Iron Chef. To the right of the entrance is a dining space featuring a sushi bar, while the basement has been outfitted with two large and small teppanyaki grill counters along with private seating. The hood of the teppanyaki counter suspended from the five-meter-high ceiling is shrouded with an iron sheet pierced with countless tiny holes. The ceiling, floor and walls are all rendered in black, and by effectively controlling the lighting, the chefs are given center stage in this space.

**一夜の舞台を思わせる
興奮と輝きに満ちたレストラン**

TV番組「料理の鉄人」の三代目和の鉄人として名声を馳せた森本正治氏が開いた店舗。入口左手には、寿司カウンターを生かしたダイニングスペースを、地下には大小二つの鉄板焼カウンターと個室が配される。5mの天井から吊り下げた鉄板焼カウンターのフードを無数の小さな穴の開いた鉄板で覆い、天井、床、壁の全てを黒くし照明をコントロールする事で、料理人がぽっかりと浮かぶステージが生まれた。

1　The private room of the first floor sushi corner
2　The first floor as seen from the first floor entrance

1　1階寿司コーナー個室
2　1階エントランスより寿司カウンターを見る

1

2F

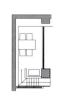

1F

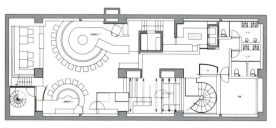

B1F

5

3 Teppanyaki grill counter of basement
4 The bar corner at the back of the first floor
5 Private seating in the teppanyaki corner of basement

3 B1階鉄板焼カウンター
4 1階バーコーナー
5 B1階階鉄板コーナー個室

restaurant morimoto XEX

Opening Hours:Monday-Wednesday, Saturday and Sunday Teppan・Sushi18:00~23:00(L.O.)Bar Drink~24:00(L.O.) Thursday and Friday and the day before National Holidays Bar Food~1:00(L.O.)Bar Drink~1:30(L.O.) Holidays:None Tel:03-3479-0065 Floor Space:618㎡ Seats:102 Opened:30/10/2005 Operated by:Y's table co., Ltd. Design:spin off co., ltd. Contractor:union planning co., Ltd. Photographs:Nacása & Partners inc.

restaurant morimoto XEX

営業時間:月~水, 土・日 鉄板・寿司18:00~23:00（L.O.）Barドリンク~24:00（L.O.）木・金・祝前日BARフード~翌1:00（L.O.）BARドリンク~翌1:30（L.O.） 定休日:無休 Tel:03-3479-0065 店舗面積:618㎡ 席数:102席 開店日:2005年10月30日 経営:㈱ワイズテーブルコーポレーション 設計:スピン・オフ 施工:㈱ユニオンプランニング 撮影:Nacása & Partners inc.

MINAGI

海凪

☐ Address：Maple Aobadai 1F, 2-11-27, Aoba-ku, Yokohama, Kanagawa
☐ Design ：STUDIO MOON / Shigeki Kaneko

☐ 住所　：神奈川県横浜市青葉区2-11-27 メープル青葉台1F
☐ 設計　：㈲スタジオムーン / 金子 誉樹

A tranquil time and space brought about by authentic materials

Tucked away in a high-class residential area in Kanagawa prefecture, Minagi entertains guests with authentic Japanese cuisine. Aiming for adults with a true sense of beauty, the restaurant is a space where customers can relax and enjoy the live fish brought in directly from the hatchery. Genuine materials have been used everywhere, from the 900-angle solid teak flooring to the specially made porcelain tiling on the walls and lighting that sways to the sound of guests' voices. The end result is a space that truly adds to the already incredible food served here.

本物の素材が生み出す安らぎの時と空間

神奈川県の高級住宅街にひっそりと佇む、本格和食料理店『海凪（MINAGI）』。真に美味しいものを知る大人をターゲットに、産地から直接仕入れる活魚等をゆったりと楽しめる空間だ。900角のムクのチーク材のフローリングに特注の陶板のタイルを貼った壁面や、人の声に反応して揺らぐ特注照明等、本物の素材を随所に使用した。提供される料理をより引き立てる空間に仕上った。

1

1 A view of the interior from the facade

2 Counter seating

3 A private room towards the back of the restaurant

1 ファサードより店内を見る

2 カウンター席

3 店内奥の個室

MINAGI

Opening Hours:17:00~24:00(L.O.23:00) Holidays:None Tel:045-983-2311 Customer:Middle 30s-Middle 50s Floor Space:107.36㎡ Seats:34(counter10, tables16, private rooms8) Opened:25/10/2005 Operated by:Yokohama Kushikobo Design:STUDIO MOON Contractor:kuukankeikaku kobo Photographs:Hiroshi Nemoto

海凪

営業時間：17:00～24:00（L.O.23:00）　定休日：無休 Tel：045-983-2311　来客者層：30代半ば～50代半ば　店舗面積：107.36㎡　席数：34席（カウンター10席、テーブル16席、個室8席）　開店日：2005年10月25日　経営：㈱横浜串工房　設計：㈲スタジオムーン　施工：㈲空間計画工房　撮影：根本 ヒロシ

NORIHIRO

のり寛

☐ Address ：The Peak1F, 2-50-13, Nakamachi, Meguro-ku, Tokyo
☐ Design ：EMC / Toshikazu Hasebe

☐ 住所 ：東京都目黒区中町2-50-13 ザ・ピーク1F
☐ 設計 ：㈲イー・エム・シー / 長谷部 俊和

Spirit of hospitality and Japanese style worked into a relaxed sophisticated hideaway

Under the guidance of Kiccho founder Teiichi Yuki, this restaurant is managed by chef Norihiro Tanaka. Located off Tokyo's busy Komazawa Street, the chef says his establishment hopes patrons will "Get away from hectic day-to-day life and enjoy their food slowly and calmly." The six-meter-high ceiling in the main dining area features a beautiful overhead fan and envelopes guests in a peaceful environment distinguished by the sound of flowing water. This is a space that makes the most of the peaceful essence of natural materials and the spirit of Japanese cuisine.

もてなしの心と和の設えに安らぐ大人の隠れ家

『吉兆』創業者、湯木貞一氏の指導を受けた料理長田中憲博氏が腕をふるう店。駒沢通り沿いにひっそりと佇み、「日頃の喧噪から離れ、ゆっくりと食事を楽しんでもらいたい」との料理長の想いが込められた。天高6mの吹き抜けと雅な扇のオブジェに目をみはるメインダイニングでは、水のせせらぎと穏やかな時がゲストを包む。自然素材の優しさと日本料理の真髄に心満たされる和みの一店となった。

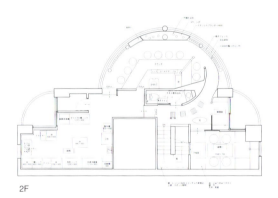

2F

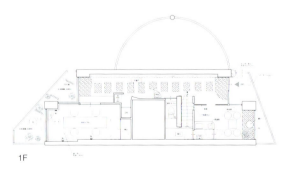

1F

1 The peaceful waiting area
2 The radiant main dining area with its unfinished wood fixtures

1 心静まる待合席
2 カウンター席の白木が眩しいメインダイニング

3 The first floor private rooms with bamboo flooring and tatami mat ceiling

4 A passageway modeled on those of Kyoto's Pontocho district features bamboo that evokes a peaceful feel

3 床に竹を天井に畳をあしらった1階個室

4 京都の先斗町をイメージした竹壁が清々しい路地風の通路

NORIHIRO

Opening Hours:Lunch12:00~14:00(entering)Dinner 17:00~21:00(entering) Holidays:Irregular Tel:03-3710-7581 Customer:Middle 40s-80s Couples living nearby, business dinner Floor Space:132㎡ Seats:20(counter 10, 2private rooms) Opened:31/3/2006 Operated by:ASIAN BREEZE Co., Ltd. Design:EMC Contractor:EMC Photographs:JPA Shooting

のり寛

営業時間:昼12:00〜14:00（入店）夜17:00〜21:00（入店）定休日:不定休 Tel:03-3710-7581 来客者層:40代半ば〜80代 近隣ご夫婦, 接待 店舗面積:132㎡ 席数:20席（カウンター10席, 個室2室／掘り炬燵式）開店日:2006年3月31日 経営:アジアンブリーズ 設計:㈲イ・エム・シー 施工:㈲イ・エム・シー 撮影:JPAシューティング

Hatagoya Jiro

旅籠屋次郎 大宮店

- Address：Kimuraya Building 2F～B1F, 1-18, Daimon-cho, Omiya-ku, Saitama-shi, Saitama
- Design ：SPACE IMD Co., Ltd. / Fumio Ichikawa

- 住所 ：埼玉県さいたま市大宮区大門町1-18 キムラヤビル2F～B1F
- 設計 ：スペース・アイエムディ㈱ / 市川 文夫

A calm space located on the former site of a Japanese-style inn

In order to prevent there developing any sense of monotony over the three floors that this establishment occupies, each space has been given its own narrative. Making your way through the old inn's entranceway, the space unfolds as an ancient Kyoto-style restaurant. Private rooms are modeled on a sake storehouse and tea house, while vivid red lacquer ware and bamboo slats set against the wall contrast with the modern cherry blossom viewing path. This is a place where various Japanese traditions are recreated to make every visit a source of wonderment.

かつての旅籠の地に甦らせた和み処

2階からB1階までの広い店内が単調にならないように、各々の空間にストーリー性を持たせて構成した『旅籠屋次郎 大宮店』。趣きある旅籠玄関をくぐると、京の老舗料亭をイメージした玄関がゲストを迎える。酒蔵を模した空間やお茶室をイメージした個室、鮮やかな紅殻壁と犬矢来のコントラストがモダンな花見小路…。様々な和の空間が魅せる店舗は、訪れる度に非日常性を楽しませてくれる場となった。

2F

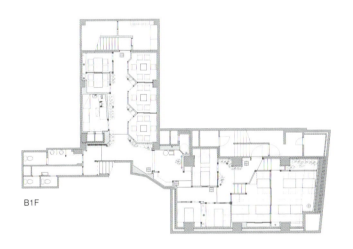

B1F

1F

1

2

1 The entrance

2 The private room modeled after a sake storehouse with its beautiful red lacquer ware

1 エントランス

2 1階　漆喰壁が美しい酒蔵を模した空間

3

3　The second floor is design to recreate a cherry blossom viewing path in Kyoto
4　A second floor private room whose walls and tables are decorated with kimono fabric creating a modern finish
5　The private rooms in the basement floor
6　The hearth seating in the basement

3　2階　京都の花見小路をイメージ
4　2階個室　壁には着物柄のパネルをテーブルには着物地を貼付けてモダンな空間を演出
5　B1階個室
6　B1階囲炉裏席

4

5

6

Hatagoya Jiro

Opening Hours:17:00~23:30 Holidays:None Tel:048-647-6365 Customer:Over20s family Floor Space:495㎡ Seats:180
Opened:5/2005 Operated by:DANKE Design:SPACE IMD Co., Ltd. Contractor:DANKE Photographs:Front Page / Masamichi
Sumiyoshi

旅籠屋次郎 大宮店

営業時間:17:00~23:30 定休日:無休 Tel:048-647-6365 来客者層:20代以降、ファミリー層 店舗面積:495㎡ 席数:180席 開店日:2005
年5月 経営:㈱だん家 設計:スペース・アイエムディ㈱ 施工:㈱だん家 撮影:㈲フロント ペイジ / 住吉 正道

018 | JAPANESE
日本料理店

Robatayaki
炉端焼

Robata JINYA

炉ばた 陣や 恵比寿本店

☐ Address ：Maizon 115 1F, 1-15-4, Ebisu, Shibuya-ku, Tokyo
☐ Design ：engine inc. / Takahiro Todoroki

☐ 住所 ：東京都渋谷区恵比寿1-15-4 メゾン115 1F
☐ 設計 ：㈲engine / 轟 貴弘

A design that uses natural wood and lighting to express the qualities of Robata cuisine

The concept behind this design was "An old Robata restaurant in a fishing village on the coast transported into the modern world." All of the wood used here is from a house in Niigata prefecture that was over 100 years old. By using the wood for chairs, tables and the counter, the lumber has been brought to life once again. Also, by foregoing ceiling illumination in favor of small standing lights on the counter, the red hot fires of the charcoal braziers appear to shine even more brightly.

「炉端焼」を演出する木材の存在感と照明計画

「海沿いの漁師町に昔からあるような炉端焼屋を現代に甦らせる」とのコンセプトのもとにデザイン。木材は全て新潟の100年以上前の古民家を解体したものを使用し、椅子、テーブル、カウンター等の家具にも利用する事で以前より存在するかのような趣きを演出した。また、天井照明を使用せず床、カウンター上に小ぶりのスタンド照明を取り入れ、備長炭が赤々と燃える炉を強調させている。

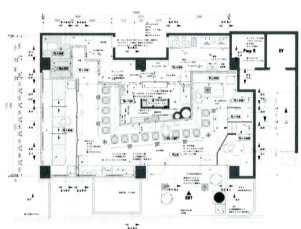

1

2

1　Two braziers and a huge red lantern spark the interest of passers by
2　The private rooms are steeped in an atmosphere of nostalgia
3　Ladles used for serving are arranged on the backs of the chairs
4　Sake bottles are lit up to make a feature on the walls

1　2台の篝火と巨大な赤提灯が通行人の好奇心を誘う入口
2　懐かしさにも似た空気が包む個室
3　椅子の背もたれ部分に配膳時に使うしゃもじをアレンジ
4　日本酒のボトルを照明にして壁のポイントに

Robata JINYA

Opening Hours:18:00～1:00 Holidays:Sunday Tel:03-3443-0577 Customer:25s-60s men and women Floor Space:89.45㎡ Seats:41(counter16, parlors25) Opened:3/3/2006 Operated by:La-brea Dining Design:engine.inc. Contractor:Oguri Cooperator:KOIZUMI LIGHTING TECHNOLOGY CORP. Photographs:Mizuho Tadokoro

炉ばた 陣や 恵比寿本店

営業時間:18:00～翌1:00 定休日:日曜 Tel:03-3443-0577 来客者層:25～60代の男女 店舗面積:89.45㎡ 席数:41席(カウンター16席、小上がり25席) 開店日:2006年3月3日 経営:㈱ラ・ブレア・ダイニング 設計:㈲engine 施工:㈱オグリ 協力:コイズミ照明㈱ 撮影:田所 瑞穂

GINZA YASUNO

銀座やす乃

□ Address：Izumo Building B1F, 8-8-1, Ginza, Chuo-ku, Tokyo
□ Design：STUDIO MOON / Shigeki Kaneko

□ 住所　：東京都中央区銀座8-8-1 出雲ビルB1F
□ 設計　：㈲スタジオムーン / 金子 誉樹

A classic space that could only be experienced in Ginza

Ginza Yasuno charms guests with its French teppan cuisine that draws on the quality of its ingredients to the fullest. The concept is "teppan savored in the modern classic atmosphere of Ginza", and the inside of the restaurant has been designed to make guests feel as if they have wandered in to a western-style house of yesteryear. In keeping with its appearance as a social hub from the good old days, the interior utilizes base colors of browns and white in order to create a relaxed atmosphere. Overall, this is an establishment that brings the highest quality of teppan grill cuisine to the mature neighborhood of Ginza.

銀座の地で体感できるクラシックな空間

素材の良さを存分に引き出す鉄板フレンチが魅力の『GINZA YASUNO』。「銀座のモダンクラシックな空間で味わう鉄板焼」というコンセプトのもと、店内のインテリアは懐かしい洋館を彷彿させるデザインに。古き良き時代の社交場を彷彿させる店内は、茶と白のカラーをベースに落ち着いた空気感を生み出す。大人の街銀座で、高級鉄板焼を食する醍醐味に満ちた一店。

1

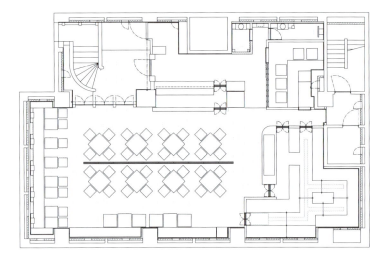

1　A view of the refined atmosphere of the entrance
2　A view of the bar counter and entrance from the interior
3　The main dining area is partitioned by removable lattice doors
4　Private counter seating

1　重厚な雰囲気が漂うエントランスを見る
2　店内よりバーカウンター、エントランスを見る
3　取り外し可能な格子戸で仕切ったメインダイニング
4　個室カウンター席

2

4

GINZA YASUNO

Opening Hours:Monday-Friday11:30~3:00 Saturday and Sunday and
National Holiday12:00~23:00 Holidays:None Tel:03-3575-9007
Customer:40s-50s Floor Space:200㎡ Seats:50 Opened:4/2005
Operated by:belluna Design:STUDIO MOON Contractor:kuukankeikaku
ko-bo Photographs:Hiroshi Nemoto

銀座やす乃

営業時間:月～金11:30～翌3:00 土・日・祝12:00～23:00 定休日:無休
Tel:03-3575-9007 来客者層:40代～50代男女 店舗面積:約200㎡ 席
数:50席 開店日:2005年4月 経営:㈱ベルーナ 設計:㈲スタジオムーン
施工:㈲空間計画工房 撮影:根本 ヒロシ

GINZA NAMIKIDORI IMAIYA SARYOU

銀座並木通り 今井屋茶寮

- Address：Royal Crystal Ginza4F, 5-4-6, Ginza, Chuo-ku, Tokyo
- Design：Merchandising Organization Co., Ltd.
- 住所　：東京都中央区銀座5-4-6 ロイヤルクリスタル銀座4F
- 設計　：㈱マーチャンダイジング・オーガニゼーション

Tranquil Japanese restaurant with simple beauty

Located on the fourth floor of a building on Ginza's famous Namiki Street, this restaurant specializes in the finest quality chicken from Northern Japan and fresh seafood such as live squid. Alighting from the elevator, guests are led through a rock garden to the dining area, hearing the sounds of Shishiodoshi, a bamboo device which is used to drive deer away. There are secluded private rooms on a slightly raised level, a main dining area decorated with an aquarium that delights one's eyes, and a large Tatami mat room suitable for large parties. While the design is simple, it makes the best use of the texture of materials like stones and woods to create a laidback atmosphere.

簡素な美に心惹かれる安らぎの日本料理店

銀座並木通り沿いのビル4階に位置し、比内地鶏の究極の焼鳥や活イカ等の新鮮な海の幸を提供する店舗。エレベーターを下りると、店内奥へと石庭が続く情緒ある空間が広がり、鹿おどしの音が耳に心地よく響く。店内は籠り感溢れる高床式離れ個室、客の目を楽しませる生け簀を配したメインフロア、そして宴会対応型の和室で構成。シンプルな中に、石や木等の素材感が生きた寛ぎの場だ。

1

3

1　The private rooms on a slightly raised level and passageway are viewed from the entrance
2　Artistic cooking manners of chefs are visible from the table seat in the main floor
3　The semi-European feel of the private rooms evoke nostalgia for the Taisho Era
4　The private rooms, featured with a fireplace with a coverlet, are let with a soothing light

1　入口より高床式離れ個室と通路を見る
2　テーブル席横では職人の手さばきも見れるメインフロア
3　大正ロマンを感じる高床式離れ個室の洋の間
4　掘り炬燵式個室には荒間障子から柔らかな光が差し込む

GINZA NAMIKIDORI　IMAIYA SARYOU

Opening Hours:Weekday Lunch11:30~14:30(L.O.14:00) Dinner17:00~23:00(L.O.22:00) Saturday and Sunday and National Holiday11:30~23:00(L.O.22:00) Holidays:None Tel:03-6215-6622 Customer:Late 20s-60s men and women, Office worker nearby Floor Space:264.9㎡ Seats:82 Opened:10/12/2005 Operated by:Food Scope, Inc. Design:Merchandising Organization Co., Ltd. Contractor:Tansei-sha Co., Ltd. Photographs:JPA Shooting

銀座並木通り 今井屋茶寮

営業時間：平日ランチ11:30～14:30（L.O.14:00）ディナー17:00～23:00（L.O.22:00）土・日・祝11:30～23:00（L.O.22:00） 定休日：無休 Tel：03-6215-6622 来客者層：20代後半～60代の男女、近隣在勤者 店舗面積：264.9㎡ 席数：82席 開店日：2005年12月10日 経営：㈱フードスコープ 設計：㈱マーチャンダイジング・オーガニゼーション 施工：㈱丹青社 撮影：JPAシューティング

TEPPAN YAKI ROKUBAN - KAN

鉄板焼ステーキ 六番館

☐ Address：Tetsuko Rokuban-cho Building B1F , 3, Rokuban-cho, Chiyoda-ku, Tokyo

☐ Design：YUSAKU KANESHIRO + ZOKEI - SYUDAN Co., Ltd. / Yusaku Kaneshiro, Miho Umeda

☐ 住所：東京都千代田区六番町3番地テツコ 六番町ビルB1F

☐ 設計：兼城 祐作十造形集団㈱ / 兼城 祐作・梅田 美穂

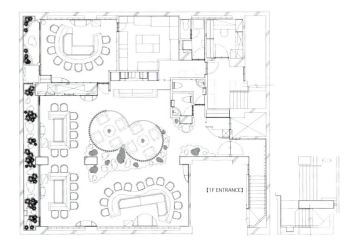

【1F ENTRANCE】

1

Welcoming atmosphere created with Japanese materials and a rock garden

This highly priced teppanyaki restaurant was designed around the theme "Japanese Garden," and the use of heavy materials, including stone and iron, gives it a sense of solidity and sophistication. Four different teppanyaki counters are set up here, with the counter and smoke intake hood cleverly integrated. In back of the grill place are luminescent Japanese paintings and stone wall, which display a yard that imparts a sense of dignity. This luxurious interior enhances the great taste of the high quality ingredients served here.

石庭が醸し出す風情ある和のマテリアルに心和む

客単価の高い高級鉄板焼という業態に合わせ「和の庭園」をテーマに、各素材に重量感のある石や鉄材を使用して空間に重厚感と高級感を与えている。4つの異なる鉄板焼カウンターを配置し、カウンターとフードのデザインを一体化させた席には、焼き場のバックに発光型の日本画や石壁の庭をディスプレイする事で品格と存在感が感じられる。高級食材の旨味をより引き立てる贅沢感溢れる空間。

| 1 | The interior as seen from the entrance | 1 | エントランスより店内を見る |
| 2 | The waiting bar | 2 | ウェイティングバー |

3	The VIP room in back of the establishment	3	店内奥のVIPルーム
4	The teppan counter with elegant straight lines	4	曲線が優美な鉄板カウンター
5	A U-shaped teppan counter	5	コの字型鉄板カウンター

TEPPAN YAKI ROKUBAN - KAN

Opening Hours:Lunch11:30~14:00 Dinner17:30~22:00 Holidays:Saturday and Sunday and National Holiday Tel:03-3264-3394 Customer:Late 30s- Early 50s Business dinner Floor Space:212.5㎡ Seats:46(one room for10, counter 28) Opened:9/3/2006 Operated by:Wiser - investment Design:YUSAKU KANESHIRO + ZOKEI - SYUDAN Co., Ltd. Contractor:Wiser Co., Ltd. Photographs:Masahiro Ishibashi

鉄板焼ステーキ 六番館

営業時間:ランチ11:30~14:00 ディナー17:30~22:00 定休日:土・日・祝 Tel:03-3264-3394 来客者層:30代後半~50代前半 接待 店舗面積:212.5㎡ 席数:46席（個室10席，カウンター28席） 開店日:2006年3月9日 経営:ワイザー・インベストメント有 設計:兼城 祐作十造形集団㈱ 施工:㈱ワイザー 撮影:石橋 昌弘

Tetsunoya
旬菜炙りと旨い酒 鐵の家

☐ Address：Noborito Tachibana Building1F , 3467-1, Noborito, Tama-ku, Kawasaki, Kanagawa
☐ Design：TENPO KENKYU-SHITSU Co., Ltd. / Shigeru Ishida

☐ 住所　：神奈川県川崎市多摩区登戸3467-1 登戸橘ビル1F
☐ 設計　：㈱店舗研究室 / 石田 茂

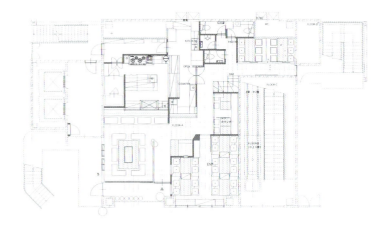

Japanese restaurant integrates into a town that protects old houses

The town of Nobuto, famed for its many vegetables and delicious sake, is inexorably linked to the many old gardens and houses within its boundaries. Considering it's the locale, this establishment decided to renovate an old building for its premises. Elements of Japan's traditional lifestyle are incorporated into the guest seating zone, while natural materials and soft lighting produce a sense of warmth throughout the space. At the back of the store, there is a sense of remove in a sunken room. Overall, this is an interior steeped in nostalgia where one can encounter forgotten Japanese culture.

古民家を守る街へ配慮をなした和食処

『旬菜炙りと旨い酒 鐵の家』のある登戸は、古民家園があるほど古民家が地元に根付いている場所。その立地を考慮し、地域に合った店舗作りを基本に古民家を再現している。日本の伝統的な生活スタイルを店舗内の客席に盛り込み、天然素材と柔らかな光で暖かな空間を創出。店内奥へ歩を進めれば、離れ感のある掘りごたつ式個室も。忘れかけていた日本の文化と懐かしさに出会える一店。

1　**2**

1　The narrow entranceway heightens visitor's sense of anticipation
2　The latticework and aged wood table in the sunken room
3　Wood with artisan's inscriptions and lacquered walls make for a relaxing vibe in the hearth seating area

1　エントランス 店内への期待感を高める細道
2　格子とエイジングしたテーブルで演出した掘り炬燵式個室
3　銘黒色の木材と漆喰壁に心落ち着く囲炉裏席

Tetsunoya

Opening Hours:17:00〜24:00(L.O.23:20) Holidays:None Tel:044-933-9332 Customer:Over 20s men and women Floor Space:92.4㎡ Seats:58 Opened:29/4/2005 Operated by:Tachibana Design:TENPO KENKYU-SHITSU Co., Ltd. Contractor:TENPO KENKYU-SHITSU Co., Ltd. Photographs:Shin Photowork / Shinji Miyamoto

旬菜炙りと旨い酒 鐵の家

営業時間:17:00〜24:00(L.O.23:20) 定休日:無休 Tel:044-933-9332 来客者層:20代以降の男女 店舗面積:92.4㎡ 席数:58席 開店日:2005年4月29日 経営:㈲橘 設計:㈱店舗研究室 施工:㈱店舗研究室 撮影:㈲シンフォトワーク / 宮本 真治

UMI

碧海

- Address：Royal Building 2F, 3-9-3, Roppongi, Minato-ku, Tokyo
- Design ：N MAEDA ATELIER / Norisada Maeda

- 住所 ：東京都港区六本木3-9-3 ロイヤルビル2F
- 設計 ：㈲前田紀貞アトリエ一級建築士事務所 / 前田 紀貞

A space unified by an R cross section for floor, walls and ceiling

Rather than dividing the three zones (counter area, private rooms and bar) with walls, this space restrainedly allows a connection between each area. A private room enveloped in leather-like material that looks as though the ceiling has been peeled back is located in the center of the space and an elliptic indent into the floor lends the sense of a mutual exchange. By focusing on this method of dividing the space, it seems possible to escape from interior design being limited to surface texture and ornamentation.

床・壁・天井をR断面の一筆書きで繋いだ空間

カウンター・個室・バーの3つのシーンを壁で仕切り孤立させるのではなく、互いのスペースに控えめな関係を生み出した空間。天井面がめくれたかのような皮膜の様なもので包んだ個室を店舗中央に浮遊させ、穿たれた楕円形の穴より双方の気配を感じる。この「空気を仕切る手法」に注目する事で、インテリアデザインという作業も表面的・装飾的な物から脱する事が可能になるかもしれない。

1

2

1 The sushi counter area
2 The bar counter seating
3 The slightly raised private rooms as viewed from the sushi counter

1 寿司カウンター席
2 バーカウンター席
3 寿司カウンターから小上がり個室を見る

UMI
Opening Hours:18:00~5:00(L.O.4:00) Holidays:Sunday and National Holidays Tel:03-5414-7758 Customer:30s-60s business dinner Floor Space:69.7㎡ Seats:25 Opened:4/1/2005 Operated by:Akio Kobayashi Design:N MAEDA ATE-LIER Contractor:BUILD Photographs:SHIN PHOTO WORK inc. / Shinji Miyamoto

碧海
営業時間:18:00～翌5:00（L.O.4:00） 定休日:日・祝 Tel:03-5414-7758 来客者層:30代～60代接待 店舗面積:69.7㎡ 席数:25席 開店日:2005年1月4日 経営:小林 秋夫 設計:㈲前田紀貞アトリエ一級建築士事務所 施工:㈱美留士 撮影:㈲シンフォトワーク / 宮本 真治

Wa Ga Ku Shi

ワガクシ

☐ Address ：4-30-29, Taishi-do, Setagaya-ku, Tokyo
☐ Design ：STUDIO NAGARE Co., Ltd. / Takahiro Yokoi

☐ 住所 ：東京都世田谷区太子堂4-30-29
☐ 設計 ：㈱スタジオナガレ / 横井 貴広

Japanese restaurant themed around recycling

In the old district of Sangenjaya, where senior residents mingle freely with far younger denizens, this Japanese restaurant targets diners in their 30s and 40s, and uses wood and white walls to evoke the ambience of a hideaway. Bearing in mind the frequency with which establishments are renovated in Tokyo, the interior uses only lumber taken from forest thinning and the extensive use of timber adds a sense of warmth to the space, and allows for recycling after it is dismantled for renovation. The warm lighting also enhances the cozy feel here.

リサイクルをテーマにした和食店の空間設計

高齢者層と若者層の文化がぶつかる下町の三軒茶屋で、30代〜40代の中年層を狙い、木と白壁の隠れ家的な雰囲気を演出した店舗。短いサイクルで改装が繰り返される飲食業界を背景とし、間伐材から取り出す角材のみで構成し、木を使用する事で温かみを出しながらも、解体後のリサイクルも考慮した空間設計だ。暖色の照明をプラスする事で十分に暖かさを感じられる空間となった。

1

3

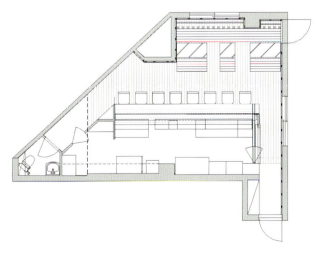

1 The warmly lit entrance
2 The rhythmical table seating constructed from timber on the horizontal and vertical
3 the counter seating and table seating

1 柔らかな光が灯るエントランス
2 垂直水平に組み上げた木がリズミカルなテーブル席
3 カウンター席とテーブル席

Wa Ga Ku Shi

Opening Hours:18:00~2:00 Holidays:Tuesday Tel:03-3411-5757 Customer:Late 20s, couple Floor Space:47㎡ Seats:18(counter 8, table10)Opened:17/10/2005 Operated by: Kazuhito Hosaka Design: STUDIO NAGARE Co., Ltd. Contractor:Hasegawa Kenko Inc. Photographs:Kunio Okoshi

ワガクシ

営業時間:18:00～翌2:00 定休日:火曜 Tel:03-3411-5757 来客者層:20代後半～ カップル 店舗面積:47㎡ 席数:18席（カウンター8, テーブル10席） 開店日:2005年10月17日 経営:保坂 和仁 設計:㈱スタジオナガレ 施工:㈲長谷川建工 撮影:大越 邦生

Yasaiya Mei

やさい家 めい

☐ Address ：Omotesando Hills 3F, 4-12-10, Jingumae, Shibuya-ku, Tokyo
☐ Design ：SWANS I.D. Co., Ltd. / Toshio Koyama

☐ 住所 　：東京都渋谷区神宮前4-12-10 表参道ヒルズ本館3F
☐ 設計 　：㈱スワンズ・アイ・ディー / 小山 トシオ

Zoning of varied rectangular spaces

The restaurant serves cuisine that features arrangements of organic vegetables. The complex space features varied rectangles that features bold counter seating that surrounds the kitchen, as well as zoning for a waiting bar and drink counter seating. The open counter seating has a demonstrative effect in that guests can see the misting in the open showcase that keeps the vegetables fresh. Various forms such as marble, wooden senbon lattice and futuristic pendants have been combined together without malaise to create what is ultimately a creative interior.

矩形が変形なスペースのゾーニング

有機野菜をアレンジした料理を提供する店。矩形が変形で複雑なスペースに、大胆にキッチンを囲むオープンカウンター席、ウェイティングバー兼ドリンクカウンター席等をゾーニング。オープンカウンター席には、野菜を新鮮に保つ霧の出るオープンショーケースを置いて、デモンストレーション効果も。大理石や木製千本格子、未来的なペンダント等種々の様式を合わせ、違和感のない独創的な空間となっている。

1

1　The entrance
2　The waiting bar and drink counter as seen from the entrance

1　エントランス
2　入口側より見たウェイティングバー兼ドリンクカウンター

4

3 Counter seating viewed from the window
4 Private seating

3 窓側より見たカウンター席
4 個室

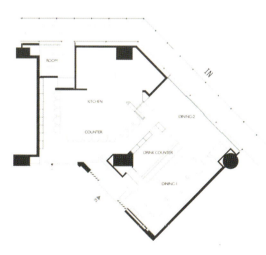

Yasaiya Mei

Opening Hours:11:00~24:00(L.O.23:00) Lunch 11:00~17:00(L.O.16:15) Holidays:None (except when Omotesando Hills is closed) Tel:03-5785-0606 Customer:Shopper, Office worker, local residents Floor Space:148.96㎡ Seats:50(bar counter 6, firesidecounter 14, tables24, private rooms6) Opened:11/2/2006 Operated by:EAT WALK Design:SWANS I.D. Co., Ltd. Contractor:TANSEISHA Co., Ltd. Photographs:Nacása & Partners inc.

やさい家 めい

営業時間:11:00～24:00（L.O.23:00）ランチ11:00～17:00（L.O.16:15） 定休日:無休（表参道ヒルズに準ずる）Tel:03-5785-0606 来客者層:表参道ヒルズを訪れる方, 近隣のビジネスマン, 在住の方 店舗面積:148.96 ㎡ 席数:50席（バーカウンター6席, 炉端カウンター14席, テーブル24席, 個室6席）開店日:2006年2月11日 経営:㈲イートウォーク 設計:㈱スワンズ・アイ・ディー 施工:㈱丹青社 撮影:Nacása & Partners inc.

UOKUNI

海鮮茶屋 魚國

☐ Address : Odawara Station Building LUSCA2F, 1-1-9, Sakae-cho, Odawara-shi, Kanagawa
☐ Design : Merchandising Organization Co., Ltd. / Tomokazu Nagao

☐ 住所 : 神奈川県小田原市栄町1-1-9 小田原駅ビル ラスカ2F
☐ 設計 : ㈱マーチャンダイジング・オーガニゼーション / 永尾 友和

A modern tea room that makes use of specialty products and the appearance of an odawara post station

The concept of this establishment is an Odawara teahouse where travelers can enjoy local viands while taking a breather from their journeys. With the image being that of a teahouse where various people passing through the station building would visit, materials such as cherry trees, earthen walls, and washi paper have been used to create a refined interior skillfully blended with contrasting modern materials such as glass and metal.This is topped off by displays of fish that is caught on the day, the freezer and "Kamado" meaning stove that cooks rice, those which one can watch processes of cooking through and convey the food culture.

宿場町・小田原の面影と特産を生かした現代の茶屋

「地域の食材を楽しみ、旅の途中で一息つける場所＝小田原茶屋」がコンセプト。小田原駅ビルに訪れるさまざまな人が立寄れる「茶屋」をイメージし、桜、土壁、和紙等の日本の伝統的な素材を、ガラスや金属などの現代的な素材と組合わせて洗練した空間を創出している。さらに、その日取れた小田原の魚を飾り、シズル感を演出するアイスベット、白米、五穀米を炊き上げる「かまど」など、それら食材を調理する過程の見える炊き場や刺し場と、食の文化も伝える。

1

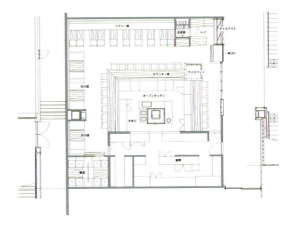

1　A view of the facade
2　The kitchen
3　Sofa-style seating as seen from the kitchen

1　ファサードを見る
2　厨房を見る
3　厨房からソファー席を見る

3

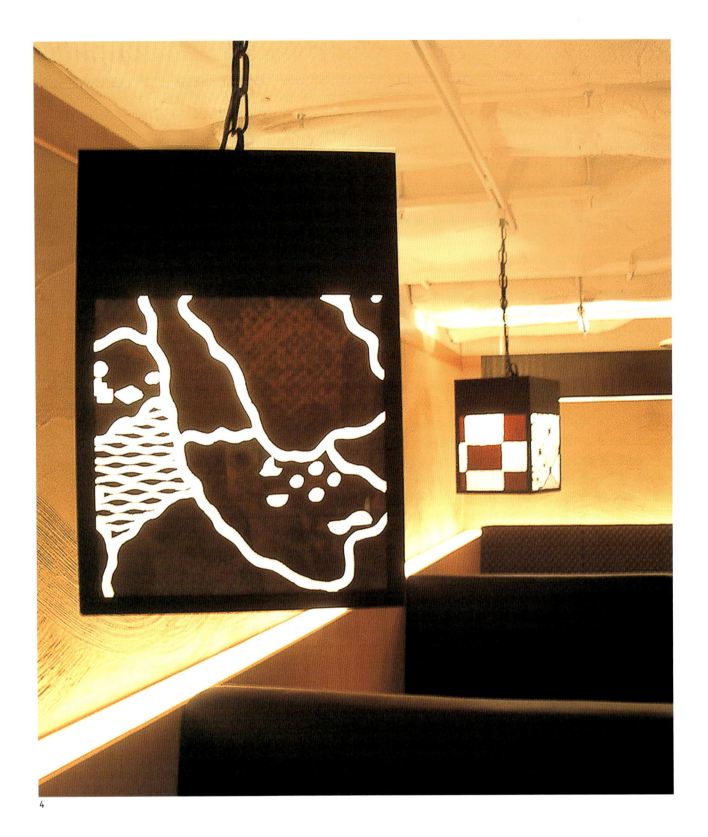

4

4 Lantern illumination using Ise-style patterned paper

4 伊勢型紙 行灯照明

UOKUNI

Opening Hours:11:00~22:00 Holidays:None Tel:046-524-1187 Customer:Tourists, Living nearby
Floor Space:147.7㎡ Seats:62 Opened:25/6/2005 Operated by:UOKUNI Design:Merchandising
Organization Co., Ltd. Contractor:Merchandising Organization Co., Ltd. Photographs:Tomokazu
Nagao

海鮮茶屋 魚國

営業時間:11:00～22:00 定休日:無休 Tel:046-524-1187 来客者層:観光客, 地域在住者 店舗面積:
147.7㎡ 席数:62席 開店日:2005年6月25日 経営:有魚國商店 設計:株マーチャンダイジング・オーガニゼー
ション 施工:株マーチャンダイジング・オーガニゼーション 撮影:永尾 友和

2 CHINESE RESTAURANTS

中国料理店

027 | CHINESE
中国料理店

Established restaurant
serving Beijing Cuisine
and Peking Duck
北京料理店、
北京ダックの老舗

ZENSHUTOKU

全聚徳 銀座店

☐ Address：Ginza World Town Building 6F, 5-8-17, Ginza, Chuo-ku, Tokyo
☐ Design ：Kenji Sugawara Architect & Associates,Inc / Kenji Sugawara

☐ 住所 ：東京都中央区銀座5-8-17 銀座ワールドタウンビル6F
☐ 設計 ：㈱菅原賢二設計スタジオ / 菅原 賢二

**A Beijing cuisine restaurant that takes the classic Shiheyuan courtyards
of China's capital city as its motif**

With 142 years of tradition and a classic Beijing theme, this restaurant has adopted the architectural style of
the iconic Shiheyuan courtyards that once symbolized China's capital city. All essence of Japanese sensibility has been removed to create a presentation that adheres to the traditions of the courtly Beijing of old.
House gates have been installed in the entrance, while the interior is composed of a hut-style roof support-
ed by cylindrical pillars and walls built of the classic tiles of Beijing. The ornamental bricks and wood lattice
windows have been arranged in original designs based on popular, time-honored Chinese patterns.

北京を代表する「四合院」をモチーフとした北京料理店

142年の歴史を持つ店舗の伝統と古への北京をテーマに、北京を代表する建築物「四合院」
の建築様式をモチーフとしている。日本的感性に訴えるエッセンスを汲み取り、伝統を踏襲しつ
つ新しくもある洗練された古への北京を表現。入口には宅門を設け、店内は円柱で支えた小屋
組みと北京古窯磚を積んだ壁で構成。壁の装飾煉瓦や窓の木格子等は、古来より中国で親
しまれている模様を基本にオリジナルの意匠を施した。

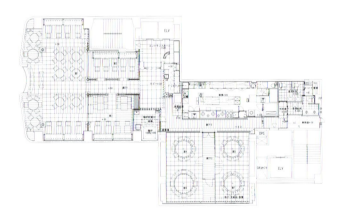

1

1　The entrance

2　The dining area is enhanced by one-hundred year old bricks and Min dynasty furnishings

1　エントランス

2　100年前のレンガや明朝家具が効いたダイニング

3 Circular private rooms for the passing of an elegant time
4 Table seating
5 The walls in the hallways feature reliefs of lotuses done in brick

3 優雅な時が流れる円卓個室
4 テーブル席
5 通路壁には蓮などの煉瓦のレリーフを施している

ZENSHUTOKU

Opening Hours:Weekday 11:30~15:00(L.O.14:30)
17:00~23:00(L.O.22:00) Saturday and Sunday National
Holiday 11:30~22:00(L.O.21:00) Holidays:None Tel:03-
5568-8668 Customer:30s-50s business dinner Floor
Space:376㎡ Seats:160(dining hall 90, private room 60)
Opened:30/10/2005 Operated by:Zenshutoku JAPAN
Design:Kenji Sugawara Architect & Associates,Inc
Contractor:DAISHIN KOUGEI Photographs:Keisuke
Miyamoto

全聚徳 銀座店

営業時間:平日11:30〜15:00(L.O.14:30)17:00〜23:00
(L.O.22:00)土・日・祝11:30〜22:00(L.O.21:00) 定休日:無
休 Tel:03-5568-8668 来客者層:30代〜50代 接待 店舗面積:
376㎡ 席数:160席(ダイニングホール90席,個室60席) 開店
日:2005年10月30日 経営:全聚徳ジャパン㈱ 設計:㈱菅原賢二
設計スタジオ 施工:大信工芸㈱ 撮影:宮本 啓介

Shiengranfon

四川中華厨房 鮮藍坊

Address：Noborito Tachibana Building 2F , 3467-1, Noborito, Tama-ku, Kawasaki, Kanagawa
Design ：TENPO KENKYU-SHITSU Co., Ltd. / Shigeru Ishida

住所 ：神奈川県川崎市多摩区登戸3467-1登戸橘ビル2F
設計 ：㈱店舗研究室 / 石田 茂

Chinese restaurant with a resort feel

The Sichuan region of China is sometimes referred to as the "Land of Abundance," and this restaurant captures the feeling of its warm climate with the design concept of "A New Resort for Sichaun." Creating the atmosphere of an open resort, the interior is designed to make visitors feel as though they are in the great outdoors. The open kitchen is modeled on a movable food stall, and the noises from the chefs at work and loud voices from the customer seating area combine to create a merry soundtrack to this unusual Chinese dining experience.

隔てのないリゾートを意識した中国料理店

モノが豊富で豊かな国という意味で「天府の国」と呼ばれる四川。気候的に暑いイメージを持ち、そこから「四川の新しいリゾート」というデザインコンセプトが生まれた。開放的なリゾート地を感じさせ、店内でありながらも外を感じるような空間作りだ。店内のオープンキッチンは「屋台」をイメージ。厨房から聞こえる声や客席での宴の笑い声が、心地良いBGM効果となるラフな空間となった。

1

2

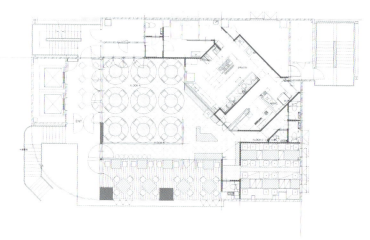

1 The signboard on the left side of the entrance
2 The open terrace area
3 The kitchen as seen from the main dining area

1 エントランス 石板を使用した外看板
2 オープンテラス
3 メインダイニングより厨房を見る

Shiengranfon

Opening Hours:Lunch11:30~15:00(L.O.14:00) Dinner 17:00~23:30(L.O.23:00) Holidays:None
Tel:044-933-9337 Customer:All target Floor Space:141.9㎡ Seats:90 Opened:29/4/2005
Operated by:Tachibana Design:TENPO KENKYU-SHITSU Co., Ltd. Contractor:TENPO
KENKYU-SHITSU Co., Ltd. Photographs:Shin Photowork / Shinji Miyamoto

四川中華厨房 鮮藍坊

営業時間：ランチ11:30～15:00（L.O.14:00）ディナー17:00～23:30（L.O.23:00） 定休日:無休 Tel:
044-933-9337 来客者層:オールターゲット 店舗面積:141.9㎡ 席数:90席 開店日:2005年4月29日
経営:㈲橘 設計:㈱店舗研究室 施工:㈱店舗研究室 撮影:㈲シンフォトワーク/宮本 真治

GINZA ASTER

中国名菜 銀座アスター ベルシ 二日比谷

☐ Address ：Toho Twin Tower Building3F , 1-5-2, Yurakucyo, Chiyoda-ku, Tokyo
☐ Design ：R&K Partners / Kiyofumi Yusa, Yasumasa Ichida

☐ 住所 ：東京都千代田区有楽町1-5-2 東宝ツインタワービル3F
☐ 設計 ：㈱R&Kパートナーズ / 游佐 清文・市田 容正

A renovation that brings a new value and personality to an already famous eatery

How does one preserve the traces of the old restaurant while bringing in the essence of the new Ginza Aster? The renovation of the restaurant answers this question with a presentation that carefully maintains the traditions of Chinese cuisine while fusing them with the food culture of Japan. Pre-existing floors, walls, ceilings, fixtures, and other parts of the old restaurant have been used wherever possible in the presentation of this new concept, which features large, divided masses of horizontal and vertical light and Chinese antiques arranged throughout the dining area in a manner reminiscent of an art museum. The final effect is a classy interior that embraces the history and heritage of this famous restaurant.

名店に新たな価値と個性を生み出す「リノベーション」

前店舗の痕跡を残しつつ如何に『銀座アスター』らしさを融合するか……。このリノベーションは、当店が中国料理の伝統を守りながら日本の食文化と融合する姿と重なる。床・壁・天井・設備等、既存の物を最大限に利用しつつ、新しいコンセプトを表現できるよう、縦の光、横の光と大きく光の塊を分け、随所に中国のアンティークを美術館の様に配置。名店の持つ歴史性と伝統が包む上質な空間となった。

1

1 The entrance
2 Translucent partitioning provides gentle division of the interior

1 エントランス
2 光を透過するパーティーションで優しく仕切る

3 A curtain of light heightens expectations of fine dining
4 Table seating
5 Round-table private seating

3 光のカーテンがダイニングへの期待を高める
4 テーブル席
5 円卓個室席

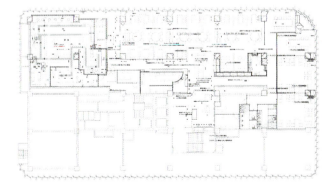

GINZA ASTER

Opening Hours:11:00~22:00 Holidays:None Tel:03-5521-1625 Customer:30s-40s Floor Space:780㎡ Seats:130 Opened:29/4/2006 Operated by:Ginza Aster Co., Ltd. Design:R&K Partners Contractor:ZYCC Corporation Yuichi Yokoyama, Masatsugu Shinozaki Photographs:Keisuke Miyamoto

中国名菜 銀座アスター ベルシーヌ日比谷

営業時間:11:00～22:00 定休日:無休 Tel:03-5521-1625 来客者層:30代～40代 店舗面積:約780㎡ 席数:130席 開店日:2006年4月29日 経営:銀座アスター食品㈱ 設計:㈱R&Kパートナーズ 施工:ジーク㈱ 横山 雄一, 篠崎 将次 撮影:宮本 啓介

GINZA ROKUMEISHUN

フカヒレ専門店 銀座鹿鳴春 銀座本店

☐ Address ：Akiike Building 1F, 1-13-8, Ginza, Chuo-ku, Tokyo
☐ Design ：Tansei Integrated Design Studio Co., Ltd. / Yusuke Kemmochi

☐ 住所 ：東京都中央区銀座1-13-8 秋池ビル1F
☐ 設計 ：㈱丹青インテグレイテッドデザインスタジオ / 釖持 祐介

Smart space balanced with sincerely prepared food

When renovating this space, the owner was aiming at a step up, towards a high quality establishment. Abiding by the philosophy of "Show what should be shown, hide what should be hidden," this simple interior seeks to achieve a pleasant feel through lighting the space between seating, white and quince space. The steel wall of the facade is composed of what looks like bundles of twigs symbolizes Chinese food and shark fin soup, from the perspective of passers by it conveys the establishment's concept in a unobtrusive way and is a piece of art that can also be viewed from the interior.

名店の真摯な料理とのバランスを保つ「きちんとした箱」

改装にあたり、オーナーが目指す次なるステップと言える「上質への転身」を表現。「見せるものは見せ、隠すものは隠す」シンプルな内装で、照明、座席間隔ともに居心地の良さを追求し、白と花梨の空間に。小枝を束ねたようなファサードのスチールウォールは「中華とフカヒレ」の象徴とし、通行人の視線を緩やかに透過しつつ、店内からも眺められる空間を引き締めるアートとなっている。

1

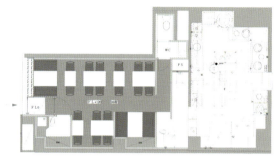

1 銀座の路地裏にひっそりと佇む
2 店のアクセントとなっているファサードのスチールウォール
3 BGMにジャズが流れる店内を見回す

1 Shanghai's location in the backstreets of the Ginza area
2 The steel wall facade that serves as an accent for the restaurant
3 The view of the interior which is filled with cool jazz music

GINZA ROKUMEISHUN

Opening Hours:11:00~14:30(L.O.)17:00~21:30(L.O.)Holidays:Sunday Tel:03-3564-5385 Customer:Women, The age layer, Business dinner Floor Space:70㎡ Seats:26 Renewal:1/5/2006 Operated by:Ryo-Commerce Design:Tansei Integrated Design Studio Co., Ltd. Contractor:D-Life Cooperator:108 Photographs:Ryota Atarashi

フカヒレ専門店 銀座鹿鳴春 銀座本店

営業時間:11:00~14:30（L.O.）17:00~21:30（L.O.） 定休日:日曜 Tel:03-3564-5385 来客者層:女性、年配層、接待 店舗面積:70㎡ 席数:26席 改装日:2006年5月1日 経営:両コマース㈲ 設計:㈱丹青インテグレイテッドデザインスタジオ 施工:㈲D-Life 協力:㈲イチ・マル・ハチ 撮影:新 良太

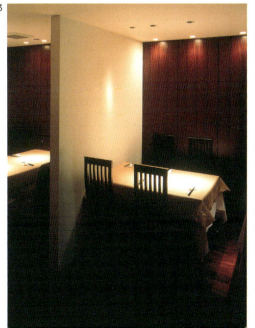

shanghai syoku

上海食

☐ Address：Atre vi Akihabara 6F, 1-9, Kandahanaoka, Chiyoda-ku, Tokyo
☐ Produce：Hiroki Kimura　　☐ Design：WEDGE.Inc / Hidefumi Takahashi

☐ 住所　：東京都千代田区神田花岡町1-9 アトレヴィ秋葉原6F
☐ 総合プロデュース：木村 宏樹　☐ 設計：㈱ウェッジ / 高橋 秀文

New Chinese restaurant with a design with female patrons in mind

This restaurant was designed as a place that bosses of the many companies located in Tokyo's Akihabara district could take their female subordinates for a treat. With a natural vibe underpinning the place, a refreshing feel is captured through the use of unfinished wood and plenty of green. Two eight-person private rooms and two for twelve are designed for small parties in mind. The walls are covered in frescoes depicting the contemporary Shanghai skyline, just one of the many details which ensure that visitors do not tire of the space easily. While red is typically the color used for the interior of Chinese dining, here green is used to appeal to young women as a new style of Shanghainese restaurant.

女性達へ発信する新しい中国料理店の意匠

秋葉原周辺に在勤の会社上司が女性部下を気軽に連れて行けるような空間デザインがテーマ。ナチュラル感を基調に、爽やかさを白木目と緑で表現。パーティ対応の8人個室を2室、12人個室を2室設け、壁面沿いは現代の上海を壁画で飾る等、随所に飽きのこないディテールを配した。中国料理のイメージを赤から緑へ進化させ、若い女性に向けて上海料理店の新たなイメージをアピールする。

1

1　The high counter seating located close to the entrance
2　The main dining area with pillars wrapped in embroidered dress fabric

1　エントランス近くのハイカウンター席
2　柱巻にチャイナドレスの生地を使用したメインダイニング

4

3　The private rooms in back with their round tables

4　The simple and modern walls

3　店内奥の円卓個室席

4　シンプルでモダンな壁面

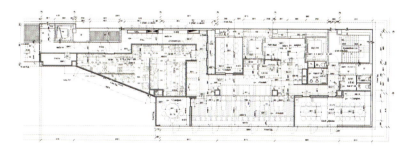

shanghai syoku

Opening Hours:11:00~23:00(L.O.22:00) Holidays:None Tel:03-5298-1186 Customer:Female office worker, Office worker, Shopper Floor Space:313.7㎡ Seats:104 Opened:1/6/2006 Operated by:GRANADA Co., Ltd. Design:WEDGE.Inc Contractor:WEDGE.Inc Photographs:Nacása & Partners inc. / Yoshifumi Moriya

上海食

営業時間:11:00~23:00（L.O.22:00）定休日:無休 Tel:03-5298-1186 来客者層:OL, サラリーマン, 買物客 店舗面積:313.7㎡ 席数:104席 開店日:2005年6月1日 経営:㈱グラナダ 設計:㈱ウェッジ 施工:㈱ウェッジ 撮影:Nacása & Partners inc. / 守屋 欣史

032 | CHINESE
中国料理店

Specialists in Tantanmen
and Mabo Rice
坦々麺と陳麻飯
(マーボーライス)専門店

CHINMA-YA Saitamashintoshin-Branch

陳麻家 さいたま新都心店

☐ Address：Keyaki Square, Shin-Toshin10, Chuo-ku, Saitama-shi, Saitama
☐ Produce：UNIVERSAL FELLOWS INC. / Hisashi Sekine   ☐ Design：Etre Design INC. / Masaki Takayama

☐ 住所　：埼玉県さいたま市中央区新都心10番地 けやきひろば
☐ プロデュース：ユニバーサル・フェローズ㈲ / 関根 久志   ☐ 設計：㈲エトルデザイン / 高山 正樹

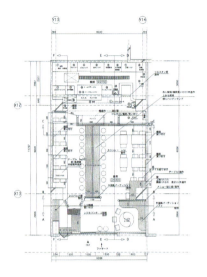

Using color and symbols to convey a strong impression

This restaurant was created with the upper ranks of the legions of office workers based in the surrounding area in mind. The color scheme is based around red, which symbolizes its top-selling sesame noodle and fried rice dishes, as well as the spicy cuisine and steamy climate of Szechwan. The balance between creating the appearance of a high-class restaurant and the prices on the menu has been carefully considered, and cute elements like Chinese furniture and symbols have been cleverly integrated into the design. The impact of the colors and symbols are intimately placed along with Chinese latticework in the narrow space which is laid out so as to be able to accommodate a single diner or large party.

強い印象を示す商品イメージカラーとシンボルマーク

近隣で働くアッパー層の会社員を意識した店作り。名物「坦々麺」と「陳麻飯」を彷彿させる赤を基調に、四川の辛さと熱気をも伝える。高級そうに見えつつ商品の値段とのバランスも考慮して、中国建具や家具、シンボルマーク等可愛い要素を上手く取り込んでいる。色とシンボルマークのインパクトが、狭い空間を程よく遮る中国格子と共に馴染み、一人客から多人数まで利用できるレイアウト。

1

1　The facade
2　The high backed Chinese-style upholstered sofas in the corner beside the entrance

1　ファサード
2　入口横の中国の布団貼りで高く上げたソファーコーナー

3 Chinese furniture has been affixed to the ceiling and counter area
4 Symbols decorate the floor at the entrance and register area

3 買いつけた中国建具をはめた天井とカウンター
4 入口床とレジ腰のシンボルマーク

CHINMA-YA Saitamashintoshin-Branch

Opening Hours:Monday-Saturday11:00~23:00(L.O.22:30) Sunday and National Holiday11:00~22:00(L.O.21:30) Holidays:None Tel:048-600-0099 Customer:20s-40s Office worker, Female office worker Floor Space:77.28㎡ Seats:54(counter18, tables36) Opened:8/9/2005 Operated by:SANSYO MANAGEMENT Inc. Design:Etre Design INC. Etre Design INC. Contractor:Yousin Inc. Photographs:Masaki Takayama

陳麻家 さいたま新都心店

営業時間:月～土11:00～23:00（L.O.22:30）日・祝11:00～22:00（L.O.21:30）定休日:無休 Tel:048-600-0099 来客者層:20代～40代のサラリーマン、OL 店舗面積:77.28 ㎡ 席数:54席（カウンター18席、テーブル36席）開店日:2005年9月8日 経営:㈱三昌マネジメント 設計:㈲エトルデザイン 施工:㈱勇進 撮影:高山 正樹

Cantonhanten
廣東飯店

- ☐ Address ：144, Yamashita-cho, Naka-ku, Yokohama, Kanagawa
- ☐ Design ：Synchronicity Co., Ltd. / Akira Kado , Masashi Otsuki
- ☐ 住所 ：神奈川県横浜市中区山下町144
- ☐ 設計 ：㈱シンクロニシティ / 角 章・大月 真司

A design that breaks away from the established styles of many shops of long standing in Chinatown

Ever since opening its doors in Yokohama's Chinatown in 1962, Canton Hanten has continued to offer customers the genuine flavor of Cantonese cuisine. With preserving the essence of the restaurant's history while bringing forth a sense of newness as the theme, the newly-remodeled first floor incorporates series of Chinese designs that symbolize the connection between the past and the future. In a bid to attract more female customers and couples, the interior is simple and strikingly clean, featuring keynotes of white and brown. This, along with the extensive use of glass throughout the store, has created a contrast between light and shadow.

中華街の老舗店に多い重厚スタイルを脱却した意匠

昭和36年横浜中華街に開店以来、広東料理を中心に本場の味を提供し続ける店。1階改装にあたり、店の歴史のエッセンスを残していかに新しさを創出するかをテーマに、過去と未来の関係性を象徴する中華図案の連なりを組み込んだ。シンプルで清潔感溢れる店内は、より女性客やカップルを取り込むよう白と茶を基調とし、ガラスを随所に使用して「光」と「影」のコントラストを生み出した。

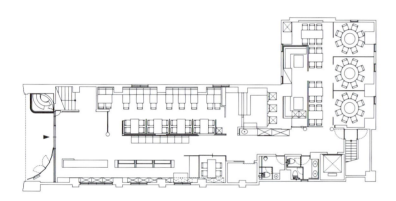

1

1　The entrance facing the main street of Chinatown　　1　中華街大通りに面したエントランス
2　Casual table seating with lunchtime traffic in mind　　2　昼食時の動線を考えてカジュアル感を出したテーブル席

3　Symbolic Chinese-style objet d'art silhouetted against a wall

4　The first floor hall featuring Chinese designs are arranged on glass

3　壁面に浮び上がるシンボリックな中華図案のオブジェ

4　1階通路　中華図案の連なりをガラス面にもアレンジ

Cantonhanten

Opening Hours:11:00~21:30(L.O.) Holidays:None Tel:045-681-7676 Customer:30s-60s men and women, couples, dinner party, business dinner Floor Space:265㎡(1F) Seats:80(1F) Renewal:24/4/2006 Operated by:Cantonhanten Design:Synchronicity Co., Ltd. Contractor:SOHO Co., Ltd. Cooperator:Yoshioka Tensou

廣東飯店

営業時間:11:00～21:30（L.O.） 定休日:無休 Tel:045-681-7676 来客者層:30代～60代の男女 カップル, 宴会, 接待 店舗面積:265㎡（1F） 席数:80席（1F） 改装日:2006年4月24日 経営:廣東飯店 設計:㈱シンクロニシティ 施工:㈱ソーホー 協力:吉岡店装

3　KOREAN RESTAURANTS

韓国料理・焼肉店

KANDA ENZO

神田 炎蔵

☐ Address：Akihabara UDX 3F, 4-14-1, Soto-Kanda, Chiyoda-ku, Tokyo
☐ Design：RIC DESIGN inc. / Teruhisa Matsumoto, Tetsuya Okabe

☐ 住所　：東京都千代田区外神田4-14-1秋葉原UDX3F
☐ 設計　：㈱リックデザイン / 松本 晃尚・岡部 哲也

Modern Japanese look applied to Edo period-style townhouse

Situated the center of the Akihabara UDX restaurant complex in the heart of the district's landmark Crossfield development, this restaurant is designed as a recreation of an Edo Period-style townhouse. Old timber beams that were used in an old house are used for the high ceiling, while square lanterns, scarlet walls, cool black slate flooring and wood slatted paper doors with graphical laser-cut patterns are all distinguishing features. This space, which mixes traditional and modern elements is forging a new attitude to dining in the popular Akihabara area.

江戸町家風の空間に広がる和モダンの魅力

「秋葉原クロスフィールド」の中核施設「秋葉原UDX」のレストラン街という立地で、あえて日本の風情を思わせる江戸の町家をイメージしている。古民家で使われていた古材の梁を渡した高い天井、スクエアな行灯、朱色の壁とクールなブラックスレートの床、木の欄間と和紙をレーザーカットしたグラフィカルな障子。伝統とモダンのレイヤーが織り成す空間は、"アキバ"の新たなダイニングシーンを担う。

1

2

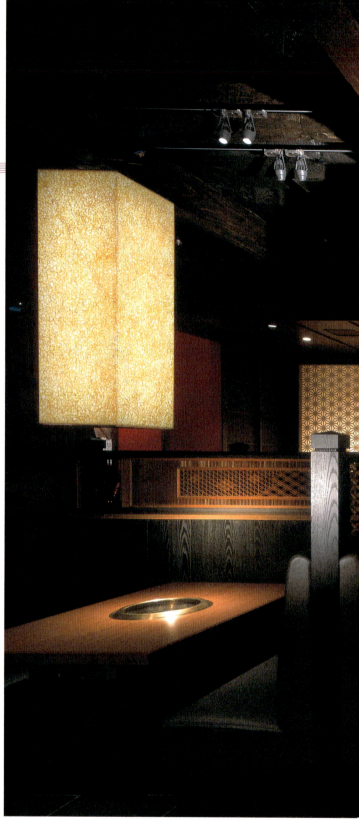

1　The facade
2　The slightly raised seating area with its smokeless roasters
3　The box seating, defined by paper lantern-style lighting and impressive cloth scrap patterns

1　ファサード
2　無煙ロースターを使用した小上がり席
3　行灯型照明&布切抜きパターンが印象的なボックス席

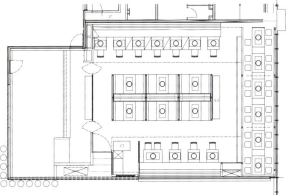

KANDA ENZO

Opening Hours:11:00~23:00 Holidays:None (except when AkihabaraUDX is closed)
Tel:03-5289-8480 Customer:Office worker, Shopper, Tourist Floor Space:163.35㎡
Seats:70 Opened:9/3/2006 Operated by:create restaurants inc. Design:RIC DESIGN
inc. Contractor:SOGO DESIGN Co., Ltd. Photographs:Nacása & Partners inc.

神田 炎蔵

営業時間：11:00～23:00 定休日：None（秋葉原UDXに準ずる）Tel：03-5289-8480 来
客者層：近隣会社員, 買物客, 観光客 店舗面積：163.35㎡ 席数：70席 開店日：2006年3
月9日 経営：㈱クリエイト・レストランツ 設計：㈱リックデザイン 施工：㈱綜合デザイン 撮影：
Nacása & Partners inc.

PAPHOUSE

ぱっぷHOUSE二子玉川

- Address：Tsuchiya Building 2F , 3-9-2, Tamagawa, Setagaya-ku, Tokyo
- Design ：T/Y DESIGN / Yasuaki Ryu

- 住所 ：東京都世田谷区玉川3-9-2 土屋ビル2F
- 設計 ：㈱ティーワイデザイン / 笠 康彰

A powerful main display playfully expressing the idea of futility

In an effort to achieve the owners aim of creating Japan's most beautiful Korean barbecue restaurant, the designers opted for beautiful-looking materials. The theme was "Futility: A Sophisticated Playfulness." Peripheral displays were kept to a minimum, being restricted to a few flourishes above the midway point of the height of the room. The main display consists of silver Japanese-style paper with ink painting, which is covered by a mirror, the glass of which has been splattered with black paint from an ink jet. The two-layered ink painting is an example of "futility" and expresses the "Sophisticated playfulness" of the theme.

「無駄」を遊び心で表するメインディスプレイの存在感

オーナーの意向である日本一綺麗な焼肉屋を目指し、綺麗が持続するような素材を心掛けているコンセプトは「無駄＝大人的遊び」。メイン以外の装飾は極力抑え、平面上での遊びや微妙な開口寸法にこだわっている。メインディスプレイは、シルバーの和紙に墨絵を施してポイントにミラーを貼り、手前のガラスにはインクジェットの墨絵を貼っている。墨絵を二層にする事で「無駄」を作り、「大人的遊び」の表現としている。

1

2

1　The interior as viewed from the entrance
2　The floor as seen from the passageway
3　A wall illuminated so as to resemble bamboo

1　エントランスより店内を見る
2　通路よりフロアを見る
3　竹をイメージしライトアップした壁面

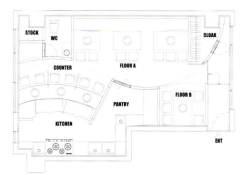

PAPHOUSE

Opening Hours:Weekday 17:00~3:00(L.O.2:00) Sunday and National Holiday17:00~23:00(L.O.22:00) Friday and Saturday and the day before National Holiday~4:30(L.O.3:30) Lunch Saturday and Sunday and National Holiday 11:30~15:00(L.O.14:30) Holidays:Irregular Tel:03-3700-1161 Customer:Late 20s Floor Space:54.8㎡ Seats:26(tables 20, counter6) Opened:3/9/2005 Operated by:Creative Connection Design:T/Y DESIGN Contractor:T/Y DESIGN Cooperator:N's Create Photographs:SHIN PHOTO WORK Inc. / Shinji Miyamoto

ぱっぷHOUSE二子玉川

営業時間:平日17:00～翌3:00（L.O.翌2:00）日・祝17:00～23:00（L.O.22:00）金・土・祝前日は翌4:30（L.O.翌3:30）ランチ土・日・祝11:30～15:00（L.O.14:30）定休日:不定休 TEL:03-3700-1161 来客者層:20代後半～ 店舗面積:54.8㎡ 席数:26席（テーブル20席、カウンター6席）開店日:2005年9月3日 経営:㈲クリエイティブ・コネクション 設計:㈱ティーワイデザイン 施工:㈱ティーワイデザイン 協力:㈱N'Sクリエイト 撮影:㈲シンフォトワーク / 宮本 真治

036	KOREAN
	韓国料理・焼肉店

Bulkogi Specialty
Restaurant
ブルコギ専門店

SURAGAN

水刺間

☐ Address ： Quiz Ebisu BuildingB1F-A, 4-3-1, Ebisu, Shibuya-ku, Tokyo
☐ Design ： SWANS I.D. Co., Ltd. / Toshio Koyama

☐ 住所 ： 東京都渋谷区恵比寿4-3-1 クイズ恵比寿ビル内B1F-A
☐ 設計 ： ㈱スワンズ・アイ・ディー / 小山トシオ

A layout based on the image of the kitchens of south Korean palaces

The name "Suragan" refers to "the place where the king's meals were prepared" during the era of the Korean Dynasties. Installed near the center of the restaurant is a fully open kitchen that allows guests to see even the cooks' feet for an even more sizzling live performance. The layout, materials, and colors have all been kept simple, with the corner detail of the walls and ceiling taking a small curve so as to bend the light and create a gentle atmosphere. Lattice doors featuring Korean paper also help to bring out the essence of the Joseon Dysnasty.

韓国宮廷の台所をイメージしたレイアウト

店名『水刺間（スラッカン）』とは、朝鮮王朝時代の「王の食事を調理する所」という意味。店のほぼ中央に厨房を配し、あえて足元が見えるフルオープンキッチンにしてより一層のライブ感とシズル感を演出。レイアウト、素材、カラーはシンプルにし、壁、天井のコーナーディテールに小さなアールを取って光を回り込ませたことにより、柔らかな空気が漂う。韓紙を貼った格子戸等で李朝の趣も出している。

1

1 The entrance hall as seen from the facade of the building
2 The open kitchen and the display of fruit liquors

1 建物ファサードから見たエントランスホール
2 オープンキッチンと果樹酒のディスプレイ

4

3 Patio seating as seen from the garden

4 Indoor seating

3 庭側から見た庭側客席

4 店内奥客席

SURAGAN

Opening Hours:17:00~1:00(L.O.24:00) Holidays:Irregular Tel:03-5447-6588
Customer:25s-40s Floor Space:159.11㎡ Seats:58(tables50, private rooms8)
Opened:24/3/2005 Operated by:Li-ga Design:SWANS I.D. Co., Ltd. Contractor:TEN-
NEN-SHA INC. Photographs:Nacása & Partners inc.

水刺門

営業時間:17:00~翌1:00（L.O.24:00）定休日:不定休 Tel:03-5447-6588 来客者層:25～
40代 店舗面積:159.11㎡ 席数:58席（テーブル50席，個室8席）開店日:2005年3月24日 経
営:㈲李家 設計:㈱スワンズ・アイ・ディー 施工:㈱天然社 撮影:Nacása & Partners inc.

HIBACHI GRILL

火鉢グリル

☐ Address：Egg BuildingB1F, 1-13-10, Jinnan, Shibuya-ku, Tokyo
☐ Design ：SKY'SCREPERS / Oouchida

☐ 住所 ：東京都渋谷区神南1-13-10　エッグビルB1F
☐ 設計 ：㈲スカイスクレパーズ / 大内田

Korean barbecue restaurant incorporates Asian resort ambience

The theme for the design of this restaurant was "A New Style of Asian Korean Barbecue." All the furniture here was hand-made in Bali, as were the hand-carved partitions between tables, the hand sculpted stone relief displayed outside the window and the Balinese Buddha images. Together they serve to conjure up the feeling of being on a resort island. The tables, doors and partitions are all made from 100-year-old Balinese timber, lending the space a natural and relaxed atmosphere.

アジアのリゾート感覚を取り込んだ 焼肉ダイニング

アジアをポイントに「新感覚のアジアン焼肉」をテーマにした店。全てバリ島で製作した手作りの家具やテーブル間に設置した手彫りによるパーテーション、大窓の外に取付けてある手彫りの石のレリーフ、バリの作家による仏陀の絵画等、本物のリゾート感覚の演出にこだわっている。また、テーブル、ドア、パーテーションはバリの100年物の木材を使用し、自然の落ち着いた雰囲気を表した。

1

1　The facade
2　The interior, with its sense of density afforded by old Balinese timber
3　The table seating area, from which Buddha images and a stone relief are visible

1　ファサード
2　バリの古材が重厚な雰囲気を生み出す店内
3　仏陀の絵画と手彫りの石のレリーフが目をひくテーブル席

HIBACHI GRILL

Opening Hours:11:30〜15:00 17:30〜23:30 Holidays:None Tel:03-5458-2800 Customer:Over 30s Floor Space:99㎡ Seats:56(all tables, private romms8) Opened:2/2005 Operated by:Y'S PROJECT Design:SKY'SCREPERS Contractor:SKY'SCREPERS Photographs:Yoshiki Hosokawa

火鉢グリル

営業時間:11:30〜15:00 17:30〜23:30 定休日:無休 Tel:03-5458-2800 来客者層:30代〜 店舗面積:99㎡ 席数:56席（全てテーブル席, 個室8名）開店日:2005年2月 経営:㈲ワイズ・プロジェクト 設計:㈲スカイス・クレパーズ 施工:㈲スカイス・クレパーズ 撮影:細川 宜樹

2

038 | KOREAN
韓国料理・焼肉店

Kamjatang Pot Dishes &
Authentic Korean Cuisine
カムジャタンなどの
鍋料理や本場韓国料理

KOREAN CUISINE ORSO

コリアンキュイジーヌ オルソ

☐ Address ：Heights Ikenoue1F, 1-27-1, Daizawa, Setagaya-ku, Tokyo
☐ Design ：T/Y DESIGN / Yasuaki Ryu

☐ 住所 ：東京都世田谷区代沢1-27-1 ハイツ池の上1F
☐ 設計 ：㈱ティーワイデザイン / 笠 康彰

With miscellany as its key feature,
this Korean restaurant fosters links to home

Gamjatang potato stew and other Korean home cooking favorites are the staple here, and the world "Miscellaneous" links to their methods of preparation. Located in a classy residential district, this Korean restaurant sought to shake off the image of its downscale peers. The walls themselves are decorated on each floor, and the design uses each room as a display space in its own right. It adds Victorian elements into Korean style, and lends a high-class feel to home cooking, and while the two are unrelated, together they serve as a link to the surrounding area.

「雑多」をキーワードに地域性に「リンク」する韓国料理店

韓国家庭料理のカムジャタン等から連想したキーワード「雑多」を軸に、高級住宅街という地域性を踏まえ、従来の韓国料理店のイメージを脱した店。テーマは「ギャップ＆リンク」。各フロアの壁自体を装飾として捉え、部屋全体をディスプレイスペースとして、デコラティブにデザインしている。韓国に対してビクトリア調、家庭料理に対して高級感。この二つが「ギャップ」であり、地域性に対する「リンク」となった。

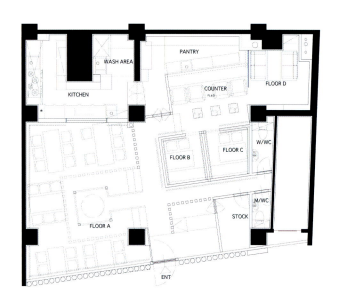

1 The facade
2 The display on the walls of the passageway
3 Movement in the kitchen as seen from the right-hand doorway on floor A

1 ファサード
2 通路壁のディスプレイ
3 フロアA　右手額縁からは厨房の動きが見れる

4 The counter seating

5 The private rooms at the back of the space; each private room has its own distinct look, based on the "Miscellaneous" theme.

4 カウンター席

5 店内奥の個室　各個室に特徴を持たせて「雑多」をアピール

KOREAN CUISINE ORSO

Opening Hours:Weekday18:00~2:00 Friday and Saturday18:00~4:00 Holidays:Monday Tel:03-5433-1088　Customer:20s-60s　Floor　Space:125㎡ Seats:42(main floor 26, counter4, 3private rooms for4) Opened:9/11/2005 Operated by:Global think system Design:T/Y　DESIGN　Contractor:T/Y　DESIGN Cooperator:N's Create Photographs:SHIN PHOTO WORK Inc. / Shinji Miyamoto

コリアンキュイジーヌ オルソ

営業時間：平日18:00～翌2:00 金・土18:00～翌4:00 定休日：月曜 Tel:03-5433-1088 来客者層:20～60代 店舗面積:125㎡ 席数:42席（メインフロア26席、カウンター4席、3個室/4）開店日:2005年11月9日 経営:㈱グローバルシンクシステム 設計:㈱ティーワイデザイン 施工:㈱ティーワイデザイン 協力:㈲エヌズクリエイト 撮影:㈲シンフォトワーク / 宮本 真治

4 FRENCH RESTAURANTS

フランス料理店

resonance

レゾナンス

- ☐ Address：Tokyo Building TOKIA 2F , 2-7-3, Marunouchi, Chiyoda-ku, Tokyo
- ☐ Design ：GLAMOROUS Co., Ltd. / Yasumichi Morita, Daisuke Watanabe(EROERO)
- ☐ 住所 ：東京都千代田区丸の内2-7-3 東京ビルTOKIA2F
- ☐ 設計 ：㈲グラマラス / 森田 恭通・渡邉 大祐（EROERO）

'Natural Luxury' emphasized by clever use of color

Vividly colored orange pendant lighting with black and white photographs printed on the inside of the shades hangs from the table seating set against the walls here. In the cozy space at the back of the restaurant is a green carpet and chairs walls on three sides are covered in mirrors, lending it an added sense of space and filling it with light. The carefully calculated color scheme and lighting, as well as the walls, illumination series of mirrors vertical lines echo the name of the establishment "resonance."

カラー使いが効いた「ナチュラル・ラグジュアリー」

壁際のテーブル席上の鮮やかなオレンジのペンダントシェード内側にはモノクロの風景写真。店内奥のグリーンのカーペットとチェアが並ぶcozyな空間は、鏡によって奥行きが与えられ、明るさも倍増する。計算されたカラースキームとライティング、そして、壁・照明・鏡等の連続する縦のラインが、『resonance』全体をすっきりと見せている。

1

1　The interior as seen from the entrance door　　1　入口ドア越しに店内を見る
2　The entrance as seen from the back of the space　　2　店内奥からエントランス方向を見る

3　The bench seating at the back of the space　　3　店内奥のベンチシート席

4　The sofa seating as seen from the windows　　4　窓の前から一番奥のソファ席を見る

4

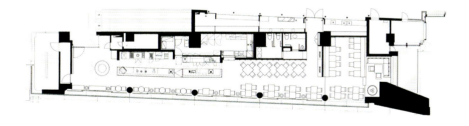

resonance

Opening Hours:11:00~15:00(Saturday and Sunday and National Holiday 11:00~16:00)
17:30~23:30(Saturday and Sunday and National Holiday 17:30~22:00) Holidays:Irregular
Tel:03-3215-7707 Customer:Late20s-40s men and women Floor Space:236.08㎡
Seats:70 Opened:11/11/2005 Operated by:Cottonclub Japan Co., Ltd. Design:GLAM-
OROUS Co., Ltd. Contractor:ISHIMARU Co., Ltd Cooperator:MAXRAY Inc., Osaka Lispel
/ Kenji Ito Photographs:Nacása & Partners inc.

レゾナンス

営業時間:11:00~15:00(土・日・祝11:00~16:00)17:30~23:30(土・日・祝17:30~22:00) 定
休日:不定休 Tel:03-3215-7707 来客者層:20代後半~40代男女 店舗面積:236.08㎡ 席数:70
席 開店日:2005年11月11日 経営:㈱コットンクラブジャパン 設計:㈲グラマラス 施工:㈱イシマル
協力:マックスレイ㈱, 大阪リスペル / 伊藤 賢二 撮影:Nacása & Partners inc.

RESTAURANT LUKE

レストラン ルーク

☐ Address：Seiroka Garden 47F, 8-1, Akashi-cho, Chuo-ku, Tokyo
☐ Produce：Yosei Kiyono　　☐ Design：YOSEI KIYONO & YO / Hiroshi Kanazawa

☐ 住所　：東京都中央区明石町8-1 聖路加ガーデン47階
☐ 総合プロデュース：清野 燿聖　☐ 設計：清野 燿聖&YO / 金澤 寛

The charm of eating in a space looking out on the sky over Tokyo

Situated 200 meters above ground, this restaurant boasts a 10.5 meter-high ceiling. When guests take their seats they take in the spectacular view of the Tokyo skyline visible at the end of a space whose floor and walls are crafted from dark wood and mirrors. The soft light that emanates from the gently swaying curtains, and the nine mirrors hanging in front of them float above the night view. The contrast between the Tokyo sky and the interior heightens the impact of the space to its greatest extent, making this seem like a restaurant that floats in the sky.

東京の空とのボーダーレスな空間で食する魅力

地上200mの高さに位置し、10.5mの天井高を持つ店内。食事の際、着席した時に視線に映り込むのは、ダークウッドとミラーで構成された床と壁の奥に広がる東京の夜景。そして、柔らかい光を放ちながら揺らめくオーガンジーカーテンと9連のミラーが、この夜景の上に浮び上がる。東京の空と店内の対比が演出力を最大限に高め、まさに天空に浮かぶレストランと言えるのではないだろうか。

1

1　The foyer
2　The guest seating, dominated by a spectacular night view

1　ホワイエ
2　煌めく夜景が空間を彩る客席

3　The bar counter

4　The terrace, which looks out on Tokyo Tower, as set up for ceremonial occasions

5　The private room as set up for wedding ceremonies

3　バーカウンター

4　東京タワーも臨めるテラス2（挙式バージョン）

5　個室（挙式バージョン）

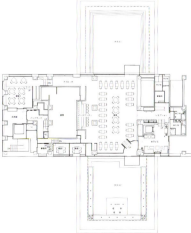

RESTAURANT LUKE

Opening Hours:11:30~15:00 18:00~22:00 Holidays:None Tel:03-3248-0211
Customer:Late 20s Floor Space:564.4㎡ Seats:96 Renewal:1/3/2006
Operated by:JR-CENTRAL PASSENGERS Co., Ltd. Design:YOSEI KIY-
ONO & YO Contractor:TSUCHIYAGUMI Cooperator:WATTS, AND WORKS
Photographs:Nacása & Partners inc.

レストランルーク

営業時間:11:30～15:00 18:00～22:00 定休日:無休 Tel:03-3248-0211 来客者
層:20代後半 店舗面積:564.4㎡ 席数:96席 改装日:2006年3月1日 経営:㈱ジェ
イアール東海パッセンジャーズ 設計:清野 燿聖&YO 施工:㈱土屋組 協力:特注照
明:㈱ワッツ ディスプレイ:㈱アンドワークス 撮影:Nacása & Partners inc.

kurkku kitchen

クルックキッチン

□ **Address**：2-18-21-1F, Jingumae, Shibuya-ku, Tokyo
□ **Design**：decorative mode no.3 inc. / Shigeki Hattori

□ 住所　：東京都渋谷区神宮前2-18-21 1F
□ 設計　：㈲デコラティブモードナンバー3 / 服部 滋樹

Space designed in harmony with nature has a message to convey

One of the five activities of kurkku, a company specializing in future lifestyles that are pleasant and kind to the environment, this restaurant is themed around the notion that "The future is in the earth," meaning that people's energy comes from food. It's like conveying the feeling of eating in the gorund, the flooring has been made lower than ground level, and layers of soil are depicted on the walls. The idea that the chefs are providing food made from safe ingredients has been worked into the design, showing how people can happily coexist with nature.

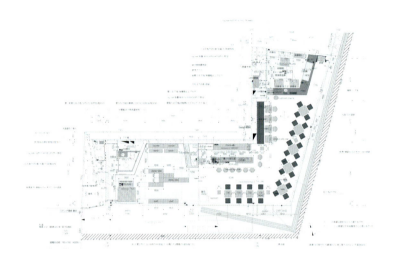

自然と調和した空間が伝えるメッセージ

快適で環境に良い未来の暮らし方を提案する『kurkku』5部門の1つ。人の活力源となる食物は土から生まれるという観点から「土の中に未来がある」との店のテーマを表した。まるで土の中で食事をするような感覚を生む店内の床は地上より低くし、壁には地層を表現。シェフ達がこだわりを持って安全な食材を提供する思いと意匠が調和し、自然と人との繋がりを伝える一店に仕上った。

1

1　The layers of soil observed on the site before construction began are depicted on the walls here　　1　壁にレストラン建築前の調査で判明した敷地の地層を表現

2 Carefully selected materials, including untreated walnut wood, are used in the interior
3 The firewood pot and coal oven used in the kitchen to bring out the best of the ingredients used

2 素材感を意識し無垢材のウォールナット等を使用した店内
3 オープンキッチン内には素材の旨味を引出す薪釜と炭炉も

kurkku kitchen

Opening Hours:17:30~23:30(L.O.22:00) Holidays:Monday Tel:03-5414-0944
Customer:Over 30s-40s men and women Floor Space:98㎡ Seats:44
Opened:21/3/2006 Operated by:kurkku Design:decorative mode no.3 inc.
Contractor:HOSOMI KOUMUTEN Photographs:JPA Shooting

クルック キッチン

営業時間:17:30〜23:30(L.O.22:00) 定休日:月曜 Tel:03-5414-0944 来客者層:30
代〜40代以上の男女 店舗面積:98㎡ 席数:44席 開店日:2006年3月21日 経営:㈲
kurkku 設計:㈲デコラティブモードナンバー3 施工:細見工務店 撮影:JPAシューティング

042 | FRENCH
フランス料理店

French-Based Italian
Cinema Restaurant
シネマレストラン、
フレンチイタリアン

copon norp

コポン ノープ

☐ Address：COPON NORP 1F・2F, 3-15-11, Jingumae, Shibuya-ku, Tokyo
☐ Design ：Nishimori Architects & Associates / Rikuo Nishimori

☐ 住所　：東京都渋谷区神宮前3-15-11 COPON NORP1F・2F
☐ 設計　：㈲西森事務所 / 西森 陸雄

Members-only cinema restaurant charms with the contrast of exterior and interior

The cinema restaurant is located in a building that was originally a beauty salon. With a row of white houses like those seen on Mediterranean islands providing inspiration for the brightly lit open space, the bright white walls and floor and spacious movable tent on the ceiling create the feeling of being outside. The adjacent dining space gives the feeling of entering a dark building from the street outside. The sight of guests enjoying their meals while they take in a movie can be seen from the open kitchen, which is separated from the courtyard area, negating any feeling of distance.

空間の内外のコントラストを演出した会員制シネマレストラン

元々美容室だった建物をシネマレストランへと増改築した店。地中海に浮かぶ島の街並みをイメージした白く明るい広場をテーマに、真っ白な壁と床、天井には開放的な可動式テントを設けた半外部的な空間だ。そこから続くダイニングは、街から暗い建物へ入ったような印象を演出。映像を楽しみつつ食事をするゲストの様子が中庭を隔てたオープンキッチンからも伺え、空間に隔たりを感じさせない。

1

1　The entrance
2　The spacious courtyard, inspired by a plaza bathed in sunlight

1　エントランス
2　自然光が溢れる広場をイメージした開放的な中庭

3   The dining area replete with 150-inch screen

4   The first floor private dining area

3   150インチスクリーンを備えたダイニング

4   1階のプライベートダイニング

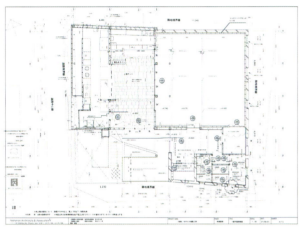

2F

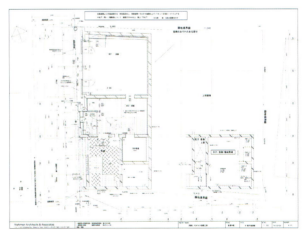

1F

copon norp

Opening Hours:14:00~2:00(L.O.23:00) Holidays:Sunday(party is possible) Tel:03-6406-3833 Customer:Those involved in the film industry 30s-50s business dinner Floor Space:227.91㎡ Seats:47(dining38, private rooms9) Opened:2/12/2006 Operated by:cafe groove Design:Nishimori Architects & Associates Contractor:Tokyu Construction Cooperator:Azu Photographs:JPA Shooting

コポン ノープ

営業時間：14:00～翌2:00（L.O.23:00）定休日：日曜（パーティ可）Tel:03-6406-3833 来客者層：映画関係者等30～50代、接待 店舗面積：227.91㎡ 席数：47席（ダイニング38席、個室9席）開店日：2006年12月2日 経営：㈱カフェグルーヴ 設計：㈲西森事務所 施工：東急建設㈱ 協力：㈱Azu 撮影：JPAシューティング

Restaurant GINTO
New York Contemporary

レストラン ギント ニューヨーク コンテンポラリー

☐ **Address**：ZOE Ginza 5F, 3-3-1, Ginza, Chuo-ku, Tokyo
☐ **Design**：age co., ltd. / Ichiro Sato , Satoshi Matsushita

☐ 住所　：東京都中央区銀座3-3-1 ZOE銀座5F
☐ 設計　：㈱エイジ / 佐藤 一郎・松下 哲

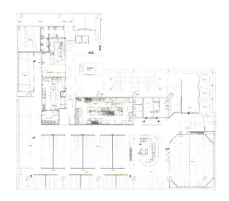

Pillars of light symbolize links to various situations

Taking into account its location in the well-heeled district of Ginza, this establishment opted to take a progression from classic to modern as its concept. Due to its large floor space and the fact that it would be used for various occasions, the design created various zones that produce a lively atmosphere despite its large scale. At the heart of the establishment is a bar area that links each of the areas and which is dynamically lit in order to best connect the disparate areas through atmosphere and detail.

光柱を取り巻く多彩なシチュエーションとの関係性

銀座という立地から正統派ディナーレストランを意識し、クラシックからモダンへの流れをコンセプトとした。店舗が広い事と幅広い用途に応える為に様々なエリアを配し、多彩なシチュエーションを演出する事で大規模でも賑わいのある空間だ。店の中心には、各エリアへの分岐点でもあるバーエリアにデザインの核となる象徴的な光柱があり、店全体の雰囲気やディテールへと繋がっていく。

1

2

4

1 The elevator hall
2 The pillars of light at the bar area
3 The main dining area
4 The interior as viewed from the passageway

1 エレベーターホールを見る
2 バーエリアの光柱を見る
3 メインダイニング
4 通路より店内を見る

Restaurant GINTO New York Contemporary

Opening Hours:Monday-Saturday11:30~23:30 Sunday11:30~23:00 Holidays:None Tel:03-3538-6600 Customer:Late 20s Female office worker, Office worker, Couples, Shopper Floor Space:647.45㎡ Seats:252 Opened:9/3/2005 Operated by:Ramla Design:age co., ltd. Contractor:TEN-NEN-SHA INC. Cooperator:NOOSA DESIGN INC. Photographs:Nacása & Partners inc.

レストラン ギント ニューヨークコンテンポラリー

営業時間:月~土11:30~23:30日11:30~23:00 定休日:無休 Tel:03-3538-6600 来客者層:20代後半~ OL, サラリーマン, カップル, 買物客 店舗面積:647.45㎡ 席数:252席 開店日:2005年3月9日 経営:㈱ラムラ 設計:㈱エイジ 施工:㈱天然社 協力:㈱ヌーサデザイン 撮影:Nacása & Partners inc.

Pierre Gagnaire à Tokyo

ピエール・ガニェール・ア・東京

☐ Address ：Minami-Aoyama Square4F, 5-3-2, Minami-Aoyama, Minato-ku, Tokyo
☐ Design ：Christian Ghion / MYU PLANNING & OPERATORS INC.

☐ 住所 ：東京都港区南青山5-3-2 南青山スクウェア4F
☐ 設計 ：デザイナー クリスチャン・ジオン / ㈱ミュープランニング アンド オペレーターズ

The "Ripple" of the Picasso of the kitchen's vision makes a wave among the people

Pierre Gagnaire à Tokyo is the most elegant and artistic one of all the three-star French restaurants, its design concept is "a single drop of water". Within its simple yet perfect form, a tiny drop of water hides infinite power. Pursuing this sort of sublimity and power of influence as a symbol for the people who visit his establishment, Gagnaire poured his spirit into the creation of this refined restaurant.

人々を触発する "厨房のピカソ" の世界を表した「波紋」

仏の三ツ星レストラン中、最もエレガントでアーティスティックな『ピエール・ガニェール・ア・東京』のデザインコンセプトは「一滴の水滴」。シンプルかつ完璧な形で、無限の力を秘めたほんの小さな存在。たった一滴の水滴が落ちた時に静寂の水面に広がる波紋をガニェール氏が追求する極致、影響力、そこに集う人々のシンボルとした、氏の精神に満ちた洗練の一店だ。

1 The view of the reception area from the bar counter
2 The dining area as seen from the entrance

1 バーカウンターから見たレセプション
2 入口から見たダイニング

3

3　Private seating

3　個室

Pierre Gagnaire à Tokyo

Opening Hours:Lunch11:30~14:00(L.O.)Dinner18:00~21:30(L.O.) Holidays:Sunday and National Holiday Tel:03-5466-6800 Customer:Over 30s Floor Space:294㎡ Seats:60(included private rooms for 6 and 9) Opened:29/11/2005 Operated by:P.G.Japan Design:MYU PLANNING & OPERATORS INC. Contractor:D.BRAIN CO.,LTD. Photographs:Masao Okamoto

ピエール・ガニェール・ア・東京

営業時間:ランチ11:30～14:00(L.O.)ディナー18:00～21:30(L.O.) 定休日:日・祝 Tel:03-5466-6800 来客者層:30代以降 店舗面積:294㎡ 席数:60席〈内個室6席、9席〉 開店日:2005年11月29日 経営:㈱P.G.Japan 設計:㈱ミュープランニング アンド オペレーターズ 施工:㈱ディー・ブレーン 撮影:岡本 成生

5 ITALIAN RESTAURANTS

イタリア料理店

045 | ITALIAN
イタリア料理店

Italian Restaurant
Bar and Bridal Cafe
イタリアンレストランバー・
カフェブライダル

CANOVIANO TOKYO/ M · TOKYO

カノビアーノ東京 / M・東京

☐ Address ：Tokyo Structure Building1F・B1F,1-9-9, Yaesu, Chuo-ku, Tokyo
☐ Design ：R&K Partners / Kiyofumi Yusa, Yasumasa Ichida

☐ 住所 ：東京都中央区八重洲1-9-9 東京建物本社ビル1F・B1F
☐ 設計 ：㈱R&Kパートナーズ / 游佐 清文・市田 容正

Bringing back memories by maintaining the old scenery of Tokyo's yaesu district

Canoviano Tokyo is located in Yaesu, a neighborhood of Tokyo that mixes elements of the old and the new. As a renovation of the first floor and basement of a building that was a completed in 1930, the first floor (originally a bank) has been resurrected as a restaurant, cafe, and chapel. The exterior visage of the building was left intact, while the interior was designed with an entirely new concept. In a contrast to the effect of the first floor, the basement office area was remade as a live music venue that is its own world of pure white. The design technique at work here is that the first floor moves in concert with time, while basement acts in opposition to it.

東京八重洲の景観の一部を担う都市の記憶を繋げる

新旧の要素が混在する街、八重洲側に位置する『カノビアーノ東京』。昭和4年竣工の東京建物の1階・地階のリノベーションを目的に、元々銀行だった1階をレストランやカフェ、チャペル等として甦らせた。外装は当時の面影を残し、内装は新コンセプトで構築。地階は事務所だった場をライブハウスとし、1階とは趣きを変えて白の世界で統一。1階は時に呼応する方法を、地階は時に対岐する方法を取っている。

B1F

1F

1

1 The classical flavor of the entrance
2 Mirrors have been affixed to the pillars to add
   a sense of length to the first floor banquet hall

1 クラシカルな趣きのエントランス
2 1階バンケット 柱にミラーを取りつけ
   奥行きを出した

3   The first floor chapel

4   The first floor cafe space

5   The basement enchants guests with the purity of white

3   1階チャペル

4   1階カフェスペース

5   白の持つ純粋さがゲストを魅了する地階フロア

5

CANOVIANO TOKYO/M・TOKYO

Opening Hours:Restaurant 11:00~14:30 18:00~23:30, Cafe 7:00~23:00, M・TOKYO18:00~6:00 Holidays:None Tel:03-6225-5491
Customer:30s-40s Floor Space:1F 1100.68㎡, B1F 678.36㎡ Seats:restaurant160, cafe30, M・TOKYO/counter18, lounge26
Opened:15/7/2005 Operated by:MOC Corporation Design:R&K Partners Contractor:Tokyo Tatemono Techno-build Co., Ltd. ZYCC
Corporation, Yuichi Yokoyama, Yorimasa Okano Cooperation:Furniture:PPM Corporation Illumination:H lighting design
Sound:Second line Photographs:Keisuke Miyamoto

カノビアーノ東京／M・TOKYO

営業時間:レストラン11:30~14:30 18:00~23:30 カフェ7:00~23:00 M・TOKYO18:00~翌6:00 定休日:無休 Tel:03-6225-5491 来客者層:
30代~40代 店舗面積:1F 1100.68㎡, B1F 678.36㎡ 席数:レストラン160席, カフェ30席, M・TOKYO/カウンター18席, ラウンジ26席 開店日:
2005年7月15日 経営:㈱モック 設計:㈱R&Kパートナーズ 施工:㈱東京建物テクノビルド, ジーク㈱横山 雄一, 岡野 頼雅 協力:家具:PPMコー
ポレーション 照明:Hライティングデザイン 音響:セカンドライン 撮影:宮本 啓介

Grotta Azzurra

グロッタアズーラ

☐ Address : Serina Green heights1F ,3-5-15, Higashi-Azabu, Minato-ku, Tokyo
☐ Design : TENPO KENKYU-SHITSU Co., Ltd. / Masami Wakayama, Mari Oishi

☐ 住所 : 東京都港区東麻布3-5-15 瀬里奈グリーンハイツ1F
☐ 設計 : ㈱店舗研究室 / 若山 昌美・大石 真里

Italian restaurant with an at-home atmosphere

Located near to a busy intersection bridge in Tokyo's upscale Azabu district, this establishment is done out like an Italian cafe, shutting out the pandemonium of the metropolis rushing by outside. The eye-catching facade is lit up in green adding a sense of width and impact. The ambience of the interior allows visitors to enjoy a lighthearted meal without being conscious of the area in which they are located. The easygoing space is divided into garden, living room and kitchen corners.

アットホームな空気感を取り込んだイタリア料理店

麻布新一の橋交差点に位置し、首都高速が近くを走る騒がしいロケーションに色を挿すべく、イタリアのカフェをイメージ。重要なファサードのアイキャッチには、グリーンを施してライトアップし、ワイド感とインパクトを与えている。店内は、麻布という地にありがながらも背伸びをせずに気軽に食事ができる雰囲気だ。ガーデン、リビング、キッチンとコーナー分けをした寛ぎの空間となった。

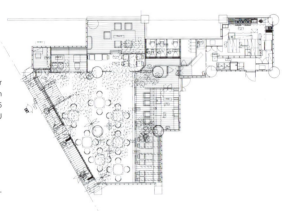

Grotta Azzurra

Opening Hours:17:00~4:00(L.O.3:30) Holidays:Irregular
Tel:03-5549-1821 Customer:Over 20s men and women
Floor Space:184.4㎡ Seats:64 Opened:19/12/2005
Operated by:r and a Design:TENPO KENKYU-SHITSU
Co., Ltd. Photographs:Masaharu Nakahashi

グロッタアズーラ

営業時間:17:00～翌4:00（L.O.3:30） 定休日:不定休 Tel:
03-5549-1821 来客者層:20代以降の男女 店舗面積:
184.4㎡ 席数:64席 開店日:2005年12月19日 経営:㈲アールアンドエー 設計:㈱店舗研究室 撮影:中橋 正治

1

| 1 | The broad frontage uses a glass door, which affords an open feel | 1 | 広い間口にガラス戸を使用して開放的なイメージを演出 |
| 2 | The table seating modeled on a spacious garden | 2 | 開放感溢れるガーデンをイメージしたテーブル席 |

047 | ITALIAN
イタリア料理店

Fixed-Course Italian
Plus Take-Out Bar
プリフィクスコースイタリアン、
テイクアウトバール併設

LA BETTOLA per tutti

ラ・ベットラ ペル トゥッティ　日本橋三井タワー店

- Address ：Nihonbashi Mitsui Tower Building B1F, 2-1-1, Nihonbashi, Muromachi, Chuo-ku, Tokyo
- Design ：Tansei Integrated Design Studio Co., Ltd. / Yusuke Kemmochi

- 住所　：東京都中央区日本橋室町2-1-1 日本橋三井タワーB1F
- 設計　：㈱丹青インテグレイテッドデザインスタジオ / 釼持 祐介

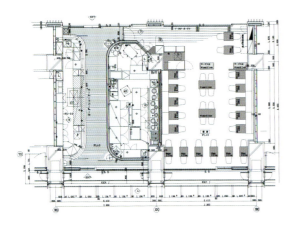

Italian restaurant designed with Nihonbashi's history and pace of life in mind

This establishment was designed to match "Edo Period Nihonbashi" the theme of the Mitsui Tower, in which is it located. On both sides of the entrance connected to the building's underground concourse are bar zones fitted with old- and new-style balustrades from Nihonbashi Bridgewhich symbolize the area's past and present. A gold-colored large wall set against the backdrop of solid objects emphasizes the restaurant's identity. The restaurant zone features faux Edo Period-style stores and latticework, as well as old tiles all arranged in a modern style which drawn attention to the establishment's concept of "Building a bridge through food culture."

日本橋の時の流れと歴史を汲むイタリア料理店

三井タワーのテーマ「お江戸日本橋」を踏襲する和の表現を汲んだ店。地下鉄コンコースとを繋ぐ両端入口に新旧の日本橋欄干を据えたバールゾーンは、古今の日本橋を象徴する。具象的なオブジェの背景に金色の大壁を配し、店のアイデンティティーを主張。レストランゾーンは江戸の商屋風に格子や瓦調のタイルでモダンな空間とし、「食文化の架け橋」という店舗コンセプトを際立たせる。

1

1　The passage to the underground concourse that is imaged "Nihonbashi"　　1　「日本橋」をイメージした通路を通り地下鉄コンコースへ

2 The modern balustrade motif   2 現在の欄干をモチーフに

3 The Edo Period balustrade motif   3 江戸時代の欄干をモチーフに

4 The bar zone sales counter   4 バールゾーンの販売カウンター

5

5   The restaurant zone, from which the kitchen is visible through latticework

5   キッチンが格子から見え隠れするレストランゾーン

LA BETTOLA per tutti

Opening Hours:11:30~21:30(L.O.) Bar 8:00~21:30(Holiday is a Sunday and National Holiday) Holiday:None Tel:03-3272-1201 Customer:Female office worker, male (Bar), Office worker (take out) Floor Space:140㎡ Seats:48(Bar standing) Opened:29/9/2005 Operated by:Ryo Commerce Design Design:Tansei Integrated Design Studio Co., Ltd. Contractor:Tanseisha Co., Ltd. Cooperator:108, Engraver:Ryuichiro Oonita, Illustrator:Hideo Wakabayashi Photographs:Ryota Atarashi

ラ・ベットラ ペルトゥッティ 日本橋三井タワー店

営業時間:11:30～21:30（L.O.）バール8:00～21:30（日・祝は定休） 定休日:無休 Tel:03-3272-1201 来客者層:OL、男性（バール）、ビジネス層（テイクアウト） 店舗面積:140㎡ 席数:48席（バールはスタンディング） 開店日:2005年9月29日 経営:両コマース㈲ 設計:㈱丹青インテグレイテッドデザイン・スタジオ 施工:㈱丹青社 協力:㈲イチ・マル・ハチ, 彫師:大仁田龍一郎, 絵師:若林秀雄 撮影:新良太

Ristorante ASO

リストランテ アソ

☐ Address：29-3, Sarugakucho, Shibuya-ku, Tokyo
☐ Design：R&K Partners / Kiyofumi Yusa

☐ 住所 ：東京都渋谷区猿楽町29-3
☐ 設計 ：㈱R&Kパートナーズ / 游佐 清文

1

A restaurant that breathes new life into a western-style house from the early days of the showa era

Ristorante ASO, which is nestled amidst the rich greenery of Daikanyama, uses as its theme the image of a Toscana Villa with Renaissance-style construction and warm pastel colors. With consideration to the importance of the garden to Florence courtyard culture, there are an abundance of corridor-connected gardens throughout the restaurant. The ceiling above the spiral staircase to the second floor is decorated with "Aozora" by fresco painter Kazumi Nukaga, creating a richly poetic space.

昭和初期の洋館に新たな生命を吹き込んだレストラン

緑豊かな代官山にある『リストランテ アソ』のテーマは、「トスカーナのVilla(邸宅)」。ルネッサンス建築様式に温かみあるパステルカラーを導入。フィレンツェの中庭文化における庭の重要性を考慮し、回廊を取入れて随所に中庭を配している。2階へと続く螺旋階段の天井には、フレスコ画家、額賀加津巳氏による「碧空-あおぞら-」を施し、詩情豊かな空間となっている。

2

1 The exterior and a 300-hundred year old zelkova tree as seen from Kyu-Yamate Street
2 The corridor from the cafe to the restaurant proper is paved in terra cotta

1 旧山手通りから店舗外観と樹齢300年の欅を見る
2 カフェからレストランへ続くテラコッタを敷き詰めた回廊

3　The main dining area looks out on a garden filled with colorful flowers

4　The impressive spiral staircase decorated by the symbolic ceiling fresco "Aozora"

3　メインダイニングより花が彩る中庭を見る

4　シンボルの天井フレスコ画（碧空）が印象的な螺旋階段

4

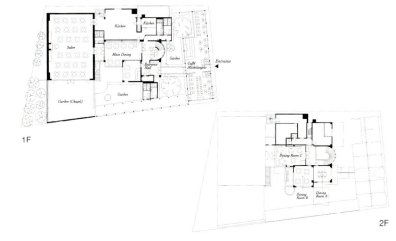

1F

2F

Ristorante ASO

Opening Hours:Lunch12:00~15:30(L.O.13:30)Dinner18:00~24:00(L.O.21:00) Holidays:Monday(closing day the next day when Monday is National Holiday) Tel:03-3770-3690 Customer:30s-40s, couple, business dinner, memorial day use Floor Space:1017.85㎡ Seats:45(maindinning, 3private rooms for4, 8,14) Renewal:11/2/2006 Operated by:Hiramatsu Inc. Design:R&K Partners Contractor:Fukuda biken Inc. Photographs:Hiroshi Tsujitani

リストランテ アソ

営業時間:ランチ12:00~15:30(L.O.13:30) ディナー18:00~24:00(L.O.21:00) 定休日:月曜(月曜祝日の場合翌日に振替) Tel: 03-3770-3690 来客者層:30代~40代、カップル、接待、記念日利用 店舗面積:1017.85㎡ 席数:45席〈メインダイニング、個室3室/ 4名、8名、14名〉 改装日:2006年2月11日 経営:㈱ひらまつ 設計:㈱R&K パートナーズ 施工:㈱フクダ美建 撮影:辻谷 宏

PASTA HOUSE
AW kitchen figlia

パスタハウス　エーダブルキッチンフィリア

☐ Address：NOB Minami-Aoyama 1F, 3-18-5, Minami-Aoyama, Minato-ku, Tokyo
☐ Design：SWANS I.D. Co., Ltd. / Toshio Koyama
☐ 住所　：東京都港区南青山3-18-5 NOB南青山1F
☐ 設計　：㈱スワンズ・アイ・ディー / 小山 トシオ

A relaxed and elegant interior composed of earth colors

AW Kitchen Figlia is located on a back street near the Omotesando crossing. As neighboring apartment buildings obstruct most outside light, the garage portion of the restaurant tends to appear gloomy even during the daytime. So, this area has been covered in a tent and made into terrace seating. The tent is made from translucent material that allows the brightness of the outdoors to pass through. The lighting scheme also takes into account the environment outside by using a mixture of HQI fixtures and halogen lamps. Aged wood has been used for the deck, while other materials include beige marble and steel.

アースカラーでまとめた落ち着きあるエレガントな空間

表参道交差点に程近い路地裏にある『AW kitchen figlia』。隣接するマンションに外光を遮られ、昼間も薄暗いイメージがあるガレージ部分をテントで覆ってテラス席とした。外部の明るさを感じられるよう、テントには光を透過する生地を使用。照明計画も外の雰囲気を考慮し、HQIとハロゲンランプの混光に。古材のデッキ、ベージュ系の大理石、スチール等の素材を生かしている。

1

3

1 The facade
2 The terrace seating and interior as seen from the terrace entrance
3 The main dining area as seen from the kitchen

1 ファサード
2 テラス入口側より見たテラス席及び店内
3 キッチン側より見たメインダイニング

PASTA HOUSE AW kitchen figlia

Opening Hours:Lunch11:00~15:00(L.O.15:00) Dinner17:30~23:00(L.O.22:00)
Holidays:None Tel:03-5772-0172 Customer:Office worker, Local residents, Those
who come to Omotesando and Aoyama for leisure Floor Space:59.76㎡ Seats:33
Opened:24/12/2005 Operated by:EAT WALK Design:SWANS I.D. Co., Ltd.
Contractor:Ogami Industry Co.,Ltd. Photographs:Nacása & Partners inc.

パスタハウス エーダブルキッチンフィリア

営業時間:ランチ11:00〜15:00（L.O.15:00）ディナー17:30〜23:00（L.O.22:00）定休
日:無休 Tel:03-5772-0172 来客者層:在勤者, 近隣住民, 表参道&青山へ遊びに来る
方々 店舗面積:59.76㎡ 席数:33席 開店日:2005年12月24日 経営:㈲イートウォーク 設
計:㈱スワンズ・アイ・ディー 施工:㈱大上工業 撮影:Nacása & Partners inc.

La Loggia
ラ ロッジア

☐ Address：San-malino Shiodome 1F, 2-4-1, Higashi-shinbashi, Minato-ku, Tokyo
☐ Design ：Ms QUESTO / Takao Inutake

☐ 住所　：東京都港区東新橋2-4-1 サンマリーノ汐留1F
☐ 設計　：㈱Ms QUESTO / 犬竹 孝雄

An oasis of greenery and sunlight in the middle of the city

As a central presence in the growing Italian neighborhood in Shiodome, with its concept of "casual and formal" La Loggia promises a diner a classy time with Italian food.Taking inspiration from New York's Il Cortile, the restaurant is composed of a dining area showered in sunlight along with a second floor bar and cigar lounge. The tables and chairs are made by Giorgetti, while the lighting fixtures are Terzani. These plus the authenticity of the ingredients used at this restaurant gives diners a real touch of Italy.

太陽光と緑で都会のオアシス感を演出

汐留にて進行中のイタリア街の中心的存在として「カジュアル＆フォーマル」をコンセプトに、豊潤な時と余韻の残るイタリア料理を提供。「ニューヨークのコルティーレ」をモチーフに、太陽の光が降り注ぐガーデンダイニング席と2階のバー＆シガーラウンジで構成される。テーブル、イスはGIORGETTI製、照明機器はTERZANI製を使用。素材の本物感と本当のイタリアらしさに触れられる一店だ。

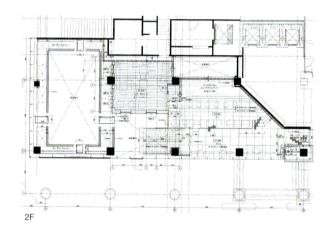

2F

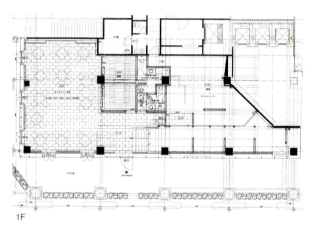

1F

1　The entrance
2　The second floor bar counter and soft drink bar
3　The garden dining seats are arranged on a floor of genuine Italian marble

1　エントランス
2　2階のバーカウンター＆ソフトドリンクバー
3　本場イタリアの大理石を床に敷いたガーデンダイニング席

La Loggia

Opening Hours:Lunch11:30~14:00(L.O.)
Dinner18:00~21:00 Bar 17:00~23:30
Holidays:Sunday and National Holiday
Tel:03-5403-0013 Customer:Female office
worker, Office worker, Family Floor
Space:390.42㎡ Seats:93(hall 48, private12,
lounge12,terrace16) Opened:14/4/2006
Operated by:Ms QUESTO Design:Ms
QUESTO Contractor:KIKORI TACHI
Photographsr:TAKAO INUTAKE

ラ ロッジア

営業時間:ランチ11:30~14:00（L.O.）ディナー
18:00~21:00 バー17:00~23:30 定休日:日・
祝 Tel:03-5403-0013 来客者層:OL、ビジネス
マン、ファミリー 店舗面積:390.42㎡ 席数:93席
（ホール48席、個室12席、ラウンジ12、テラス16）
開店日:2006年4月14日 経営:㈱Ms QUESTO
設計:㈱Ms QUESTO 施工:㈲きこりたち 撮影:
犬竹 孝雄

Milano Cucina

ミラノクッチーナ

☐ Address：Yuraku Building 1F, 3-13-1, Kyobashi, Chuo-ku, Tokyo
☐ Design：BAUHAUS MARUEI Co., Ltd. / Kiyoshi Wada , Hiroyasu Ogura

☐ 住所　：東京都中央区京橋3-13-1 有楽ビル1F
☐ 設計　：㈱バウハウス丸栄 / 和田 清・小椋 裕恭

A restaurant designed to play to feminine sensibilities

As a new concept reflecting Milano Cucina's original sense, the restaurant has been redesigned with a flavor reminiscent of the Italian region of Tuscany. While aimed mainly at women, the interior has been created to be simple and appealing to anyone. While ornamentation such as the semi-arches and ceiling painting monuments appear forebodingly high-class, careful forethought has been made to ensure that the atmosphere is still comfortable and accessible to guests. The final effect is a warm eatery scented in the spices of Italy that manages to be lively yet relaxing at the same time.

女性の感性を主とした店舗演出

『ミラノクッチーナ』独自のセンスを反映した新コンセプトとして、「イタリアトスカーナ地方」をテーマに演出をしている。女性を中心にしながらフルターゲットに受け入れられるようシンプルな空間構成とし、半アーチに空間天井絵のモニュメント等を施して上質でありつつも普段使いのできる安らぎと心地良さを配慮。イタリアの香りをスパイスに、落ち着きのある中にも賑やかで温かな店舗となった。

1

2

1　The restaurant from the outside
2　Blinds are used to provide a moderate division of space
3　The table seating and ceiling as seen from the counter seats

1　店舗外観
2　程よく空間を仕切るブラインドを利用
3　カウンター席より天井画とテーブル席を見る

Milano Cucina

Opening Hours:Lunch 11:30~14:30 Dinner 17:00~22:00 Holidays:Sunday and National Holiday Tel:03-3563-3302 Customer:Office worker, Female office worker, Local residents Floor Space:97㎡ Seats:50 Renewal:1/11/2005 Operated by:BHO Co., Inc. Design:BAUHAUS MARUEI Co., Ltd. Contractor:TAISEI ROTEC Co., Ltd. , BAUHAUS MARUEI Co., Ltd. Photographs:BHO Co.,Inc.

ミラノクッチーナ

営業時間:ランチ11:30~14:30ディナー17:00~22:00 定休日:日・祝 Tel:03-3563-3302 来客者層:近隣サラリーマン、OL、住民 店舗面積:97㎡ 席数:50席 改装日:2005年11月1日 経営:㈱ボー 設計:㈱バウハウス丸栄 施工:大成ロテック㈱建築部、㈱バウハウス丸栄 撮影:㈱ボー

ENOTECA D'ORO

エノテカドォーロ

☐ Address ：1-9-3, Hirakawa-cho, Chiyoda-ku, Tokyo
☐ Design ：TENPO KENKYU-SHITSU Co., Ltd. / Shigeru Ishida

☐ 住所　：東京都千代田区平河町1-9-3
☐ 設計　：㈱店舗研究室 / 石田 茂

Capturing the meaning of the name Enoteca: A place to drink and cellar for wine

Enoteca D'oro is situated in among a row of office buildings. With the concept of being a "wine cellar," it uses a color scheme based around the unifying color beige, which is designed to convey the attraction of traditional Italy and lend a sense of composure and dignity, highlighted by sunburst orange, which represents the hot Italian sun. The space is also distinguished by its having done away with the boundary between kitchen and dining seating, and the decoration of the walls with objects that represent windows, which lend the interior a spacious feel.

店名『エノテカ』が表す「酒場」「酒蔵」を表現

オフィスが立ち並ぶ平河町にある『ENOTECA D'ORO』。「ワイン蔵」をコンセプトに、イタリアの伝統的な魅力を出すようベースカラーをベージュ等の中間色を用いて落ち着きと重厚感を出しつつ、イタリアの光＝太陽を表すオレンジをポイントカラーに。さらに、客席とキッチンの境を無くして空間を一体にし、壁には窓をイメージしたオブジェを飾る事で、開放感も出している。

1

2

1 The entrance which conjures up the image of a wine shop with its own cellar
2 Numbered floorboards evoke a retro feel
3 The establishment's wine, its pride and joy, is displayed in style

1 エントランス。ワイン蔵のあるワイン店をイメージ
2 レトロ感を出すよう品番違いの床板を使用
3 見せる手法を取り自慢のワインを壁面に配置

ENOTECA D'ORO

Opening Hours:11:30~15:00(L.O.14:30) 17:00~23:30(L.O.22:30) Holidays:Sunday and National Holiday Tel:03-3221-8222 Customer:Over 30s men and women Floor Space:87.6㎡ Seats:42 Opened:17/1/2006 Operated by:METIUS FOODS Co., Ltd. Design:TENPO KENKYU-SHITSU Co., Ltd. Contractor:TENPO KENKYU-SHITSU Co., Ltd.

エノテカドォーロ

営業時間:11:30～15:00（L.O.14:30）17:00～23:30（L.O.22:30）定休日:日・祝 Tel: 03-3221-8222 来客者層:30代以降の男女 店舗面積:87.6㎡ 席数:42席 開店日:2006 年1月17日 経営:㈱メティウス・フーズ 設計:㈱店舗研究室 施工:㈱店舗研究室

053 | ITALIAN
イタリア料理店

Pizzeria & Bar
ピッツェリア&バール

chiocciol@pizzeria

キオッチョラ・ピッツェリア

☐ Address ：Akihabara UDX 1F, 4-14-1, Soto-Kanda, Chiyoda-ku, Tokyo
☐ Design ：Tansei Integrated Design Studio Co., Ltd. / Junichi Hasumi

☐ 住所 ：東京都千代田区外神田4-14-1 秋葉原UDX1F
☐ 設計 ：㈱丹青インテグレイテッドデザインスタジオ / 蓮見 淳一

Beautiful arched ceiling connects two different spaces

Themed around the juxtaposition of classic and modern styles, the pizzeria is divided into two spaces dominated respectively by a stand-up bar and open kitchen. The bar area features retro-look red bricks and silver mosaic tiles which make for a stylish contrast, while the pizzeria side is distinguished by classically formed arches extravagantly inlaid with gold mosaic tiles. The arched ceiling linking the two spaces is defined by the gradation of silver and gold mosaic tiles which serve to unify them.

2つの空間をつなぐ優美なアーチ型折上天井

「クラシック&モダン」をテーマに、立ち飲みのバールエリアと石窯を配したオープンキッチン形式のピッツェリアで構成。バールはレトロなレンガとシルバーのモザイクタイルを対比させ、ピッツェリアは古典的なフォルムのアーチ梁にゴールドのモザイクタイルという豪華な仕上がりだ。2エリアを繋ぐアーチ型折上天井は、モザイクタイルをグラデーション貼りし、空間を一つに融合している。

1

1　The facade
2　The standing bar, with refrigeration for preserved meats on the right

1　ファサード
2　バールカウンター横の熟成庫は商品のアピールに効果的

4

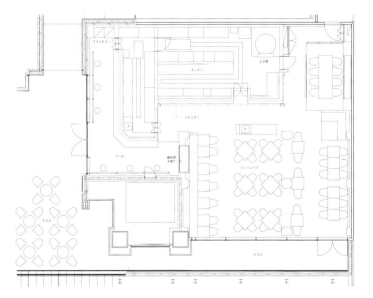

3 The integrated space, enveloped by the wine cellar
4 The pizzeria seating, framed by the gold arched ceiling overhead

3 ワインセラーと一体化したビッグテーブル席
4 アーチ梁が空間の広がりを演出するピッツェリア

chiocciol@pizzeria

Opening Hours:11:00~23:30 Holidays:None Tel:03-3258-5671 Customer:Female office worker, office worker Floor Space:178.2㎡ Seats:100 Opened:9/3/2006 Operated by:KUMAGAI Co., Ltd. Design:Tansei Integrated Design Studio Co., Ltd. Contractor:Tanseisha Co., Ltd. Photographs:Vista JAPAN Setsuo Hirosaki

キオッチョラ・ピッツェリア

営業時間:11:00~23:30 定休日:無休 Tel:03-3258-5671 来客者層:OL、ビジネスマン 店舗面積:178.2㎡ 席数:100席 開店日:2006年3月9日 経営:クマガイコーポレーション㈱ 設計:㈱丹青インテグレイテッドデザインスタジオ 施工:㈱丹青社 撮影:ヴィスタジャパン 廣崎 節雄

AQUA RESTAURANT&BAR LUXIS

054 | ITALIAN
イタリア料理店

Italian & Bar
イタリアン&バー

ラグシス

☐ Address：ZAIN EBISU Building B1F, 1-7-3, Ebisu-Nishi, Shibuya-ku, Tokyo
☐ Design ：Soi / Akihiko Shioji

☐ 住所 ：東京都渋谷区恵比寿西1-7-3 ZAIN EBISU BLD.B1F
☐ 設計 ：㈲ソーイ / 塩地 あきひこ

A design that blends a restaurant with a theater-like atmosphere

Luxis presents diners with a peaceful interior space like an oasis built around the keywords of "casual" and "gorgeous". Eyes will be drawn to the enormous 5X6 meter aquarium and hearts will be thrilled by the excitement of the conceptual service and space that blends the real and the fantastic. Guests are brought down from the entrance into an unbelievably huge cave that leads to a ruined castle-like entryway to a mysterious and soothing underwater space. The contrast between the luxurious dining area and the scenery floating around it ensure that is a restaurant that is full of surprises.

劇場の舞台的感覚と飲食店の融合をデザイン

「カジュアル&ゴージャス」をテーマに、オアシスのような癒しの空間を演出する『LUXIS』。目を奪う5×6mの巨大な水槽、実像と虚像が織りなす空間とサービスに胸ときめく「ドキドキ感」がコンセプト。地階には入口からは想像がつかない広大な空洞が広がり、廃虚風な導入から神秘的な表情で癒す水中スペースへとゲストを誘う。ラグジュアリーな店内と流れるシーンの対比で驚きに満ちた一店。

1

1 Looking down upon the main dining area

2 The bar counter continues even down the steps to the basement

3 Private seating next to the bar counter partitioned by glass

1 メインダイニング全体を上から見下ろす

2 地階への階段を降りると、バーカウンターが続く

3 ガラスのパーテーションで仕切るバーカウンター横の個室

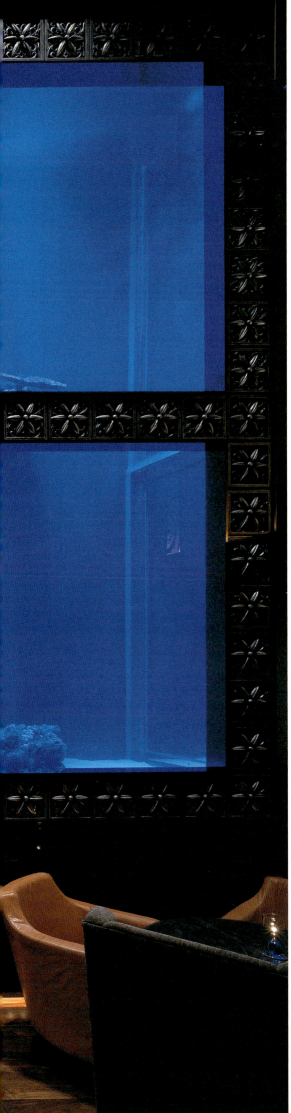

4 Nearly 300 different species of tropical fish swim freely in the aquarium in the main dining area

5 The gorgeous atmosphere of the VIP room

4 約300種の熱帯魚が自由に泳ぐメインダイニングの水槽

5 ゴージャスな雰囲気のVIP ROOM

AQUA RESTAURANT&BAR LUXIS

Opening Hours:11:00~16:00(reservation required) 16:00~6:00(usually)
Holidays:None Tel:03-5428-2288 Customer:Fashionable executives
Floor Space:206.89㎡ Seats:180(counter 12, tables 80, sofa 90)
Opened:11/7/2005 Operated by:JAPAN CHICKEN FOOD SERVICE Ltd.
Design:Soi Contractor:HATTORI LTD. Photographs:SHIN PHOTO
WORK Inc. / Shinji Miyamoto

フグシメ

営業時間:11:00~16:00(要予約)16:00~翌6:00(通常) 定休日:無休 Tel:
03-5428-2288 来客者層:高感度な大人の男女 店舗面積:206.89㎡ 席数:
180席(カウンター12席, テーブル80席, ソファ90席) 開店日:2005年7月11日
経営:㈱ジャパンチキンフードサービス 設計:㈲ソーイ 施工:ハットリ㈱ 撮影:㈲シ
ンフォトワーク / 宮本 真治

CAFÉ J-P'

カフェ ジェイピー

☐ Address：1-4-21, Takanawa, Minato-ku, Tokyo
☐ Design：NONSCALE CORPORATION / Yasuyo Hori

☐ 住所　：東京都港区高輪1-4-21
☐ 設計　：ノンスケール㈱ / 堀 育代

An enjoyable bistro cafe where one can appreciate art

With the store concept of based on the health-conscious New York-style delicatessen, NYC-based artist John Paul Philippe chose mustard yellow as a base color. Featuring a plant-like motif, his unique world view is colored by various works of art for diners to enjoy. The small space has been on divided rhythmically into three spaces (cafe, dining, and lounge), creating a warm and gentle interior full of brilliant flowers.

アートに包まれながら楽しむビストロカフェ

健康を重視したNYスタイルのデリカテッセンという店舗概念のもと、NY在住アーティスト、ジョンポール・フィリピ氏がマスタードカラーを基調色に選択。植物をモチーフに構成する彼独特の世界観が店内を彩り、様々なアートを楽しめる。小スペースにリズムを与えるように3つのシーン（カフェ・ダイニング・ラウンジ）で区切り、"はんなり"華のある優しく温かみある空間となっている。

1

1　The exterior
2　Swaying candles above the murals and iron partitions

1　外観
2　ミューラルや鉄のパーティション上に揺れる蝋燭が個性的

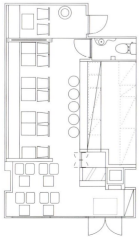

CAFÉ J-P

Opening Hours:10:00~24:00 Holidays:None Tel:03-5423-4130 Customer:Late 20s~30s female office worker, 40s housewives Floor Space:42.9㎡ Seats:24 Opened:28/4/2005 Operated by:PORTFOLIO Inc. Design:NONSCALE CORPORATION Contractor:SEMBA CORPORATION Photographs:JPA Shooting

カフェ ジェイピー

営業時間:10:00~24:00 定休日:無休 Tel:03-5423-4130 来客者層:20代後半~30代の働く女性, 40代の主婦層 店舗面積:42.9㎡ 席数:24席 開店日:2005年4月28日 経営:ポートフォリオ㈱ 設計:ノンスケール㈱ 施工:㈱船場 撮影:JPAシューティング

Trattoria & Pizzeria Zazza

トラットリア＆ピッツェリア ザザ

☐ Address：Omotesando Hills3F, 4-12-10, Jingumae, Shibuya-ku, Tokyo
☐ Design ：spin off co., ltd. / Etsuko Yamamoto

☐ 住所　：東京都渋谷区神宮前4-12-10 表参道ヒルズ本館3F
☐ 設計　：スピン・オフ / 山本 英津子

A traditional Italian restaurant with a modern presentation

Planned at the dining establishment in Omotesando Hills, Trattoria & Pizzeria Zazza features a layout composed of a central antipasto counter, plus a ham cellar, main kitchen, pizza oven. At the rear are a drink bar and wine cellar. While all these may be separate from each other, they are all actually part of the same deep oven kitchen. The versatile area around the counter can be used as a casual standing space, while the private seating in the wine cellar allows it to accommodate a variety of different occasions.

イタリアの伝統的なレストランを現代的に表現

表参道ヒルズの飲食区間に計画され、アンティパストカウンターを中心にハムセラーやメインキッチン、ピッツァ窯を、背面にはドリンクカウンターとワインセラーをレイアウト。各々が独立しつつも一つの奥行きあるオープンキッチンとして存在する。カウンター周辺にはより気軽なスタンディングスペース等にも使用可能な空間、ワインセラー奥には個室が設けられ様々なシーンに対応できる。

1

2

1　The facade. The interior can be seen from the common use corridor
2　The antipasto counter is brimming with personality
3　The main dining area in the back of the restaurant

1　ファサード 共用通路より店内を見る
2　臨場感溢れるアンティパストカウンター
3　店内奥のメインダイニング

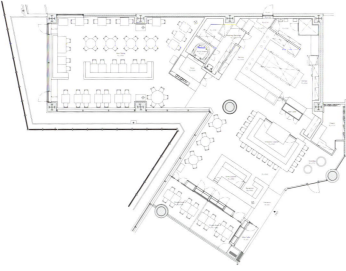

Trattoria & Pizzeria Zazza

Opening Hours:11:00~24:00 Holidays:None Tel:03-5785-1665 Floor Space:375㎡
Seats:115 Opened:11/2/2006 Operated by:Y's table.co.,Ltd. Design:spin off co.,
ltd. Contractor:Takashimaya Space Create Co., ltd. Photographs:Shinichi Sato

トラットリア&ピッツェリア ザザ

営業時間:11:00~24:00 定休日:無休 Tel:03-5785-1665 店舗面積:375㎡ 席数:115
席 開店日:2006年2月11日 経営:㈱ワイステーブルコーポレーション 設計:スピン・オフ 施
工:高島屋スペースクリエイツ㈱ 撮影:佐藤 振一

IL CHIANTI

IL CHIANTI　立川店

☐ Address：Glow Building 1F・2F,2-2-18, Shibasakicho, Tachikawa-shi, Tokyo
☐ Design：STUDIO MOON / Masateru Hirano

☐ 住所　：東京都立川市柴崎町2-2-18 グロービル1F・2F
☐ 設計　：㈲スタジオムーン / 平野 雅照

A modern Italian restaurant presented with Japanese flavor

Il Chianti Tachikawa attracts the eyes of customers with its large sign and impressive wine cellar. With the concept being "Japan as seen by a foreigner", Japanese materials have been used throughout the interior to create a skillful collection of strong color contrasts. In particular, the vermillion red counters stand out vividly as soon as one steps into the restaurant. Other features such as old pillars and folk art, as well as Towada stone and gleaming tables covered in washi paper help to cement the Japanese presentation.

和素材が演出するモダンなイタリアンレストラン

大きな店名ロゴとワインセラーが通行人の目をひく『IL CHIANTI 立川店』。「外国人から見た日本」をコンセプトに、和の素材をふんだんに使って強い色彩のコントラストを上手くまとめ上げた。一歩店内に足を踏み入れると、漆を意識した朱赤のカウンターが鮮やか。その他、古柱や日本の古民具、十和田石、光る和紙貼りのテーブル等、様々な要素を絡めて「日本」を演出している。

1

1　The exterior
2　A view of the impressive vermillion counters on the first floor
3　Table seating on the second floor features lively ink art on the walls

1　外観
2　1階　朱赤の印象的なカウンター席を見る
3　2階　壁面の墨アートが躍動的なテーブル席

3

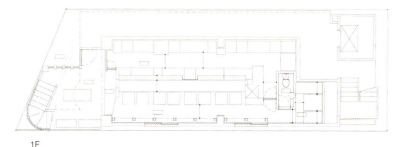

1F

2F

IL CHIANTI

Opening Hours:Lunch 11:30~16:00 (L.O.15:30) Dinner17:30~24:00(L.O.23:00) Sunday~23:00(L.O.22:30)
Holidays:None Tel:042-548-8380 Customer:20s-60s Floor Space:165㎡ Seats:39 Opened:18/4/2006 Operated
by:NAUGHTY Co.,Ltd. Design:STUDIO MOON Contractor:P.I. ARCHTECTS DESIGN Photographs:Hiroshi Nemoto

IL CHIANTI　立川店

営業時間:ランチ11:30～16:00（L.O.15:30）ディナー17:30～24:00（L.O.23:00）日曜～23:00（L.O.22:30）定休
日:無休 Tel:042-548-8380 来客者層:20代～60代 店舗面積:約165㎡ 席数:39席 開店日:2006年4月18日 経
営:㈱ノーティー 設計:侑スタジオムーン 施工:ピー・アイ・建築デザイン 撮影:根本 ヒロシ

058 | ITALIAN
イタリア料理店

Italian, Edo-style sushi
and New creation
Japanese food
イタリアン、江戸前寿司と
新創作和食

RISTORANTE RUBY ROPPONGI

リストランテ ルビー 六本木

☐ Address：GRACE 1F・2F, 7-13-7, Roppongi, Minato-ku, Tokyo
☐ Produce：Hiroki Kimura　☐ Design：WEDGE.Inc / Hidefumi Takahashi

☐ 住所　：東京都港区六本木7-13-7 GRACE1F・2F
☐ 総合プロデュース: 木村 宏樹　☐ 設計:㈱ウェッジ / 高橋 秀文

Charming space light symbolizes fusion of food culture and connection of time

Located on the ground floor across from Tokyo superclub Velfarre, this Italian restaurant was designed with theme "Magnificent Place for Social Interaction." The fusion of Italian and Japanese food culture is expressed through light and materials. The central passageway running through the main dining area resembles the stone paved roads leading to ancient Rome, and the gentle lighting that reflects and transmits this stone sparkles. The seating, which represents a fusion of Japanese and Italian aesthetics, and the Japanese-inspired counter area offer something like a trip through a time tunnel, frazzle the mind along with this splendorous space.

光が食文化の融合と時の繋がりを象徴する魅惑空間

六本木ヴェルファーレ前のビル1階に位置する店舗。テーマは「華麗なる社交場」。イタリアンと日本の食文化の融合を光と素材で表現。メインダイニングのセンター通路は石畳の古代ローマへの道を彷彿させ、石の反射と透過する柔らかな光が煌めく。イタリアと日本を共存させた席、和の表情のカウンター等、タイムトンネルを抜けるような体験は、華麗な空間とともに脳裏に焼きつく。

1

1　A view of the reception area
2　The beautiful dining seating along the 36-meter passage of light

1　レセプションを見る
2　36mに及ぶ光の通路が美しいダイニング席

2F

3　The dinig in the sushi zone
4　The second floor area dedicated to wine and cigars
5　A helmet in traditional Japanese rusted silver

3　SUSHIゾーンのダイニング
4　2階はワインとシガーをゆっくり楽しめるゾーン
5　兜を添えて日本の「いぶし銀」を表現

1F

RISTORANTE RUBY ROPPONGI

Opening Hours:Italian 17:30~1:00(L.O.) SUSHI Bar & Dining Wine lounge 17:30~5:00(L.O.)
Holidays:Sunday Tel:03-5414-2332 Customer:Later20s-Later50s rich, foreigner Floor Space:344.67㎡
Seats:96(Italian38, lounge14, SUSHI Bar & Dining44) Opened:28/4/2006 Operated by:FAIRNESS CRE-
ATION CO., LTD. Design:WEDGE.Inc Contractor:ability creation co., ltd. Photographs:Nacása &
Partners inc. / Yoshifumi Moriya

リストランテ ルビー 六本木

営業時間:イタリアン17:30~翌1:00(L.O.) SUSHI Bar & Dining ワインラウンジ17:30~翌5:00(L.O.) 定休日:
日曜 Tel:03-5414-2332 来客者層:20代後半~50代後半 富裕層、外国人 店舗面積:344.67㎡ 席数:96席(イ
タリアン38席、ラウンジ14席, SUSHI Bar & Dinig44席) 開店日:2006年4月28日 経営:㈱フェアネスクリエイショ
ン 設計:㈱ウェッジ 施工:㈱アビリティークリエーション 撮影:Nacása & Partners inc. / 守屋 欣史

LUXOR MARUNOUCHI

ルクソール 丸の内

☐ Address：Tokyo Building TOKIA 2F , 2-7-3, Marunouchi, Chiyoda-ku, Tokyo
☐ Design ：Tansei Integrated Design Studio Co., Ltd. / Taisuke Kamigaichi

☐ 住所　：東京都千代田区丸の内2-7-3 東京ビルTOKIA2F
☐ 設計　：㈱丹青インテグレイテッドデザインスタジオ / 上垣内 泰輔

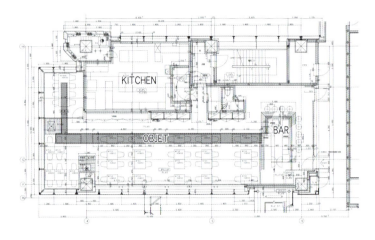

Interior furnished with objects that represent the chef's philosophy

This is the second restaurant of Italian-born chef Mario Fritolli, who creates cuising based on the traditional dishes of his native Tuscany. His culinary skills are presented as a philosophy of cooking that can be summarized as "Carving: That which is chipped away," and "Ironwork: That which is polished," both of which are represented by striking objects suspended from the ceiling. The space against which these objects are set is a pure white - like a plate before food is served on it - and represents "A vision of the future of dining in Marunouchi."

シェフの哲学を象徴したオブジェが彩る店内

総料理長マリオ・フリットリ氏のリストランテ2号店。氏の故郷であるイタリア、トスカーナ地方の伝統料理をベースにした品を提供する。シェフのスキルを「料理の哲学」とし、「削ぎ落とすもの＝彫刻」と「磨きあげるもの＝アイアンワーク」の天吊りオブジェで大胆に表現。オブジェの背景となる空間は、真っ白なお皿のようにシンプルで快適な「丸の内の食堂の将来像」をイメージしている。

1

2

1　The entrance sign, which is incorporated into the architecture of the building
2　The unfinished wood counter and entrance where carving and art is displayed
3　The relationship between neatly ordered tables and haphazardly arrange artworks

1　ビルの一部を利用したサインが光るシンプルなファサード
2　白木カウンターと一枚のアートが迎えるエントランス
3　約5mの天井を誇る開放的なダイニングとオブジェを見る

LUXOR MARUNOUCHI

Opening Hours:Lunch11:00~15:00(L.O.14:30) Dinner17:30~23:00(L.O.22:30)
Sunday and National Holiday17:30~22:00(L.O.21:30) Holidays:None Tel:03-6212-
6900 Customer:Female office worker, Office worker Floor Space:219.3㎡
Seats:65(included Bar counter 6) Opened:11/11/2005 Operated by:atlux Co., Ltd.
Design:Tansei Integrated Design Studio Co., Ltd Contractor:Tanseisha Co., Ltd.
sculpture・Iron work Maio-108 Photographs:Nacása & Partners inc.

ルクソール 丸の内

営業時間:ランチ11:00～15:00（L.O.14:30）ディナー17:30～23:00（L.O.22:30）日・祝
17:30～22:00（L.O.21:30）定休日:無休　Tel:03-6212-6900　来客者層:OL、サラリーマ
ン 店舗面積:219.3㎡ 席数:65席（内バーカウンター6席） 開店日:2005年11月11日 経
営:㈱アトリュークス 設計:㈱丹青インテグレイテッドデザインスタジオ 施工:㈱丹青社 彫
刻・アイアンワーク:Maio-108 撮影:Nacása & Partners inc.

6　PUBS

居酒屋・ダイニングバー

060 | PUBS
居酒屋&ダイニングバー

Tapas Cuisine Using
Ingredients from
Satoyama
里山素材を使ったタパス料理

Satoyama Bar
Ginza Kamadogami

里山バル 銀座竈神

☐ Address ：Ginza Building B1F , 3-3-12, Ginza, Chuo-ku, Tokyo
☐ Design ：Tansei Integrated Design Studio Co., Ltd. / Taisuke Kamigaichi

☐ 住所 ：東京都中央区銀座3-3-12 銀座ビルディングB1F
☐ 設計 ：㈱丹青インテグレイテッドデザインスタジオ / 上垣内 泰輔

Connecting people with food through a hearth god motif

Located on an alley in Tokyo's upscale Ginza district, Satoyama Bar serves healthy food from the Satoyama region and Spanish-style tapas created with lovingly gorwn ingredients also from that part of the world. Centered around the Japanese hearth god, who also is the guardian of the kitchen, this design documents the owner's borderless, timeless aesthetic and philosophy. A gallery has been established in a section that cannot be used for customer seating on the first floor, part of a proposal to create a new mutually beneficial relationship between art and restaurants.

竈神をモチーフに人々の食と繋がりの大切さを願う

銀座3丁目の路地を入る『里山バル 銀座竈神』は、体に優しい里山料理と、里山素材を工夫したスパニッシュタパスを提供する日本のバル。台所の神様である竈神を中心に、オーナーの感覚と哲学が時代と国籍を飛び超える様子をデザインでドキュメントしている。客席として利用不可能な部分には、1㎡のギャラリーを設置したり等、美術家と飲食店の「応援し合う新しい関係」を提案する。

1

1　The entrance, inspired by a mountaintop tea house, set in a gap between buildings
2　A key is displayed set into a wall behind which runs a staircase

1　銀座の裏通りビルの隙間に峠の茶屋の佇まいで構えるファサード
2　換気扇の穴を利用した窓から階段の壁に掛けられた鍵を見る

3 A hearth god motif at the back of the bar counter

4 The interior as viewed from the entrance at the bottom of the stairs

3 バールカウンターのバックに取り付けられた竈神を見る

4 地下店舗よりエントランス（階段の下がり口）を見る

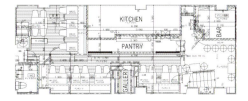

Satoyama Bar Ginza Kamadogami

Opening Hours:Monday-Friday12:00~15:00 17:30~23:30 Saturday and National Holiday12:00~23:00 Holidays:Sunday Tel:03-5524-5712 Customer:20s- 50s Floor Space:91.14㎡ Seats:39 Opened:26/10/2005 Operated by:KANOU-YA FOOD SYSTEMS Co., Ltd. Design:Tansei Integrated Design Studio Co., Ltd. Contractor:Boushakeikaku Co., Ltd. Engraver:Ryuichiro Oonita, ART:KUMO-EDITION × DAME-DISGN Photographs:Nacása & Partners inc.

里山バル 銀座竈神

営業時間：月〜金12:00〜15:00 17:30〜23:30 土・祝12:00〜23:00 定休日：日曜 Tel:03-5524-5712 来客者層：20代〜50代 店舗面積：91.14㎡ 席数：39席 開店日：2005年10月26日 経営：㈱叶家フードシステムズ 設計：㈱丹青インテグレイテッドデザインスタジオ 施工：㈱房舎計画工房 彫師：大仁田 龍一郎 ART:KUMO-EDITION × DAME-DISGN 撮影：Nacása & Partners inc.

UO DANA YOKOHAMA TSURUYA - UOTSURU

魚店 横浜鶴屋 魚鶴

☐ Address : Yokohama Sports Plaza 1F, 2-13-6, Tsuruya-cho, Kanagawa-ku, Yokohama-shi, Kanagawa
☐ Design : YUSAKU KANESHIRO + ZOKEI - SYUDAN Co., Ltd. / Yusaku Kaneshiro , Miho Umeda
☐ 住所 : 神奈川県横浜市神奈川区鶴屋町2-13-6 ヨコハマスポーツプラザ1F
☐ 設計 : 兼城 祐作十造形集団㈱ / 兼城 祐作・梅田 美穂

Objects used to tell the story of restaurant tied to local district

The owner personally stocks the kitchen with fresh fish and other produce from a market, and that fact has informed the interior design here. In the entrance space drum can tables lend an adventurous vibe to the design's take on the deep sea, and in back dynamic stained glass fish sculptures dominate the scenery. A U-shaped counter constructed from huge pieces of timber allows guests to witness the preparation of their meals and heighten their anticipation of the fresh seafood soon to be served. This establishment's unique design firmly distinguishes it from chain restaurant competitors.

一目で業態が分かるオブジェを生かした地域密着型店

オーナー自らが、市場で食材を仕入れる鮮魚等をお得に味わえる店。エントランス空間では、ドラム缶をテーブルに見立てて退廃的な深海へのアプローチをイメージしつつ、店内奥には躍動的な魚のオブジェを施している。板場を囲むコの字カウンターでは、調理過程を露出し、新鮮な魚料理がサーブされる期待感を煽る。チェーン系居酒屋とは一線を画し、個性を際立たせたインパクトある意匠。

1

2

3

4

1　The arresting facade of this street-level establishment
2　The waiting and standing bar counter area
3-4　The stunning stained glass fish sculptures

1　一際目を引く路面店『魚鶴』のファサード
2　ウェイティング＆スタンディングカウンター
3-4　店舗を象徴する魚のオブジェ

6

5 The dynamic counter area made from large logs
6 The table seating beside the counter area

5 ダイナミックな丸太の半割りのカウンター
6 カウンター横のテーブル席

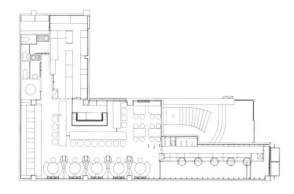

UO DANA YOKOHAMA TSURUYA - UOTSURU

Opening Hours:17:00~23:30 Holidays:None Tel:045-323-1654 Customer:30s-40s Office worker, Female office worker Floor Space:155.64㎡ Seats:85(Seats 75, Standing10) Opened:31/10/2005 Operated by:Asahi Beer Restaurant Design:YUSAKU KANESHIRO + ZOKEI - SYUDAN Co., Ltd. Contractor:TRY Co., Ltd. Photographs:Masahiro Ishibashi

魚店 横浜鶴屋 魚鶴

営業時間:17:00~23:30 定休日:無休 Tel:045-323-1654 来客者層:30代～40代ビジネスマン, OL 店舗面積:155.64㎡ 席数:85席（着席75席, 立飲み10）開店日:2005年10月31日 経営:㈱アサヒビヤーレストラン 設計:兼城 祐作十造形集団㈱ 施工:㈱トライ 撮影:石橋 昌弘

FUGA

風雅

☐ Address：FLEG Nakameguro3 RF, 1-20-2, Aobadai, Meguro-ku, Tokyo
☐ Design：Takatori kukan keikaku / Kunikazu Takatori

☐ 住所　：東京都目黒区青葉台1-20-2 FLEG中目黒3　RF
☐ 設計　：㈱高取空間計画 / 高取 邦和

Fun ways to enjoy food born from the contrast between interior and rooftop

The awkward garden space in the center of this establishment was put to best use by making it a route to the roof, rather than just for show. On the three floors that comprise this restaurant, outdoor staircase leads up from the ground floor like a ship's ladder, leading into the hot "galley" area where the food is enjoyed, or up to the roof, where customers can take in the beauty of the sky. This contrast is the establishment's greatest charm, and the movement of the clientele itself becomes a source of fun. Up on the roof, pao-style private rooms give diners the exciting feeling of being "inside while you're outside."

店内と屋上の対比が生み出す食の様々な楽しみ方

店中央にあるレンタブル比の悪い中庭を、見る庭ではなく屋上への昇降空間として設計。店舗のある3階へは、外階段を地上から船外タラップのように上がり、船内（店）では、熱気あるキッチンで食を愉しみ、屋上では空の開放感を満喫できる。この対比が最大の魅力で、客の動きが自然に発生し楽しみ方に変化が出る。屋上のパオ風個室は"外の室内"を感じ、この空気感が客をエキサイトさせる。

1

1　The Pao-style rooms allow occupants to take in their surroundings　　1　外の気配も感じるパオ風個室内を見る
2　The Pao-style private rooms on the rooftop space　　2　屋上スペースにあるパオ風個室

FUGA

Opening Hours:Weekday18:00~4:00 Sunday and Monday and National Holiday18:00~24:00 Holidays:None Tel:03-5784-1900 Customer:Young to Adult Floor Space:73.29㎡ Seats:56(3F High counter 24, sofa14, RH private room for 18) Opened:4/11/2005 Operated by:FAPS Co., Ltd. Design:Takatori kukan keikaku Contractor:Nissho Inter Life Co., Ltd. Cooperator:DAIKO ELECTRIC Co., Ltd.

風雅

営業時間：平日18:00～翌4:00日・月・祝18:00～24:00 定休日：無休 Tel:03-5784-1900 来客者層:若年層から大人の方々 店舗面積:73.29㎡ 席数:56席（3階ハイカウンター24席、ソファー14席、RH個室18名）開店日:2005年11月4日 経営:㈱ファプス 設計:㈱高取空間計画 施工:㈱日商インターライフ 協力:大光電機㈱

MAIMON GINZA

マイモン ギンザ

☐ Address ：Nishi-Tsuchihashi Building 1F・2F, 8-3, Ginza, Chuo-ku, Tokyo
☐ Design ：cafe co. / Yoshiyuki Morii

☐ 住所　：東京都中央区銀座8-3 西土橋ビル1F・2F
☐ 設計　：㈱カフェ / 森井 良幸

Dining destination designed to capture the beauty of dancing water

Maimon Ginza is primarily an oyster restaurant that also serves seafood and charcoal grilled meats. The open kitchen has been designed to offer different vies from both inside and out, and the wave design that dominates the interior makes it easy to recognize the ingredients that it is so proud of. Here artists were given a prominent role in the creation of the interior: Painter Kotaro Fukui has created paintings of ostriches for the furniture on the second floor hallway, while Hirofumi Kitao has contributed apple sculptures and painted partitions.

水の七変化を思わせる意匠が店内を包むダイニング

牡蠣を中心に魚介、肉類の炭火焼を供する『MAIMON GINZA』。キッチンは全てオープンで内・外装に対しての見え方を考慮し、店内に施した波のデザインは主力商品を程よく認識させる。また、日本画家の福井江太郎氏が2階通路の建具のダチョウの絵を、北尾博史氏が1階リンゴアートやテーブル席パーティーションを手掛ける等、アーティスト参加で店内の意匠をまとめている。

1

2

1　The facade, as viewed from straight on
2　The bar counter at the entrance frontage, as seen from the outside
3　The table seating right at the back of the first floor; boxed seating on the left

1　正面から見たファサード
2　外から見える入口正面のバーカウンター
3　1階一番奥のテーブル席 左手はボックスシート

6

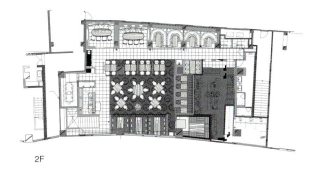

2F

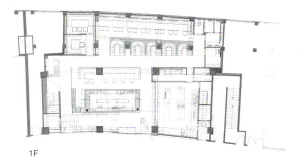

1F

4 The table seating in the center of the second floor
5 The table seating incorporated into the tablet design on the second floor
6 The private tatami mat room located near the hearth at the rear of the second floor bar counter

4 2階中央テーブル席
5 2階額の意匠の中のテーブル席
6 2階バーカウンター奥の囲炉裏を設置した個室の座敷

MAIMON GINZA

Opening Hours:Monday-Friday17:30~4:00 Saturday and Sunday17:30~24:00
Holidays:None Tel:03-3569-7733 Customer:Over 30s Floor Space:581.9㎡
Seats:150 Opened:19/4/2005 Operated by:Foodscope Co., Ltd. Design:cafe co.
Contractor:Pinc Forest Co., Ltd. Cooperator:WISE・WISE Inc., YAGI
Photographs:Nacása & Partners inc.

マイモン ギンザ

営業時間:月～金17:30～翌4:00 土・日17:30～24:00 定休日:無休 Tel:03-3569-7733
来客者層:30代以降 店舗面積:581.9㎡ 席数:150席 開店日:2005年4月19日 経営:㈱
フードスコープ 設計:㈱カフェ 施工:㈱パイン・ファレスト 協力:㈱ワイス・ワイス ㈲八木製作
所 撮影:Nacása & Partners inc.

KOSHIKAWA HENRI

こしかわHENRI

☐ Address ：Miyuki Heights1F, 4-26-2, Shimo-Ochiai, Shinjuku-ku, Tokyo
☐ Design ：STUDIO NAGARE Co., Ltd. / Takahiro Yokoi

☐ 住所 ：東京都新宿区下落合4-26-2 幸荘1F
☐ 設計 ：㈱スタジオナガレ / 横井 貴広

Japanese-style space makes use of existing pillar division

Situated in a quiet residential area, this restaurant occupies what was originally a wooden residential property. By retaining the original pillars that divide the space, the interior is long and narrow. Using predominantly white materials at the front and black in back, the space is divided by color the facade part's lattice frontage and glass framework door that sandwiches the veranda make for a gradated finish for the inside and outside. The dimly lit space there over the windowsill very bright light is effectively used to emphasize a very different feel to that of surrounding establishments, making it the area's standout destination.

既存の柱割を生かした和空間

閑静な住宅街に位置する店舗は、元々木造住宅だった物件を、既存の住宅の柱割をそのまま生かして改装したもの。細長い形の店内は、手前は白、奥は黒を基調とした素材で色彩的に仕切り、室内と屋外はファサード部分の格子扉と縁側を挟んだガラスの框戸で段階的に仕切った。そこにできた曖昧な空間は、窓越しに過度な照明効果で主張する他店舗とは異なる意味で、街並に存在感をアピールする。

1

2

1 The facade with latticework doors closed
2 When clear a latticework doors; to a guest room
3 The counter seating area with its beautiful gradated lighting
4 The Japanese-style room

1 格子扉を閉めた外観
2 格子扉を開くと客室へ
3 光のグラデーションが美しいカウンター席
4 和室

KOSHIKAWA HENRI

Opening Hours:17:00~24:00 Holidays:Monday Tel:03-3536-1495 Customer:Late 20s men and women, 30s-40s women, Local People Floor Space:45.6㎡ Seats:15(counter7, parlor8) Opened:17/12/2005 Operated by:Kazuo Komiyama Design:STUDIO NAGARE Co., Ltd. Contractor:Art-Daikuya Cooperator:Hasegawa Kenko Inc. Photographs:Nacása & Partners inc.

こしかわHENRI

営業時間:17:00～24:00　定休日:月曜　Tel:03-3536-1495　来客者層:20代後半の男女, 30代～40代の女性, 地元の方々 店舗面積:45.6㎡ 席数:15席（カウンター7席, 座敷8席）開店日:2005年12月17日 経営:小宮山 一雄 設計:㈱スタジオナガレ 施工:㈲長谷川建工 協力:㈱遠藤照明 撮影:Nacása & Partners inc.

Saraku by komeraku

お茶漬けダイニング 茶らく by komeraku

☐ Address ： Keio Fuchu Shopping Center East Mall Shoku-butai-tudumi, 1-3-6, Fuchumachi, Fuchu-shi, Tokyo
☐ Design ： ozi design works inc. / Ryosuke Hashimoto , Atsushi Handa

☐ 住所 ：東京都府中市府中町1-3-6 京王府中ショッピングセンター東モール 食舞台つづみ
☐ 設計 ：オジデザインワークス㈲ / 橋本 亮介・半田 敦司

A fusion of products and design targeting a broad age range

Specializing in a rice and green tea dish, Saraku is designed to accommodate a wide range of customers needs, with casual table seating and a raised seating area for a more laidback vibe suitable for alcohol consumption. The raised seating area uses thick cushions to achieve the feeling of being seated on a chair in a traditional tatami mat room and is a style that is comfortable for both young and old. Multifaceted pendant lamps are just one of the many Japanese-style elements incorporated into this modern design, and their red light casts an illusory glow that creates an intimate atmosphere.

幅広い年齢層を対象とした商品とデザインの融合

お酒を飲めてお茶漬けも楽しめる『茶らく』は、カジュアルなテーブル席からゆっくり飲める小上がり席と、様々なシーンに対応可。小上がり席は、厚めの座布団を使う事で椅子の感覚を持った座敷とし、若い方から年配の方にも馴染みやすいスタイルだ。切り子を使ったペンダントライト等、和の要素を持ちつつもモダンで今を感じる意匠で、その赤い明かりが幻想的で密な空気感を生み出している。

1

1 The facade
2 The raised area with its glowing pendant lamps
3 A panoramic view of the interior focusing on the raised seating area

1 ファサード
2 切り子のペンダントライトが煌めく小上がり席
3 店内全景　店内中央は小上がり席

Saraku by komeraku

Opening Hours:11:00~23:00(L.O.22:30) Holidays:None Tel:042-352-5250 Customer:20s-30s men and women Floor Space:79.50㎡ Seats:40 Opened:31/3/2006 Operated by:TUB associates Co.,Ltd. Design:ozi design works inc. Contractor:MR SERVICE Co.,Ltd. Cooperator:KOIZUMI SANGYO Co.,Ltd. Photographs:Kanta Ushio

お茶漬けダイニング 茶らく by komeraku

営業時間:11:00~23:00（L.O.22:30） 定休日:無休 Tel:042-352-5250 来客者層:20代～30代男女 店舗面積:79.50㎡ 席数:40席 開店日:2006年3月31日 経営:㈱T.U.Bアソシエイツ 設計:オジデザインワークス㈲ 施工:㈱MRサービス 協力:小泉産業㈱ 撮影:牛尾 幹太

2

KAGURAZAKA SHUN AOYAMA

神楽坂SHUN 青山

☐ Address ：2-26-9 , Minami-Aoyama, Minato-ku, Tokyo
☐ Design ：Kamiya Design Inc. / Toshinori Kamiya
☐ 住所 ：東京都港区南青山2-26-9
☐ 設計 ：㈱神谷デザイン事務所 / 神谷 利徳

A warm Japanese interior meant for passing quiet times

This establishment is located in a three story house found down the Baisouin bamboo lane located off of Aoyama's Route 246. After heading down the blind alley of the first floor with its flowing water, guests come upon the counter and table seating backed by Japanese lacquer walls. The second floor has been prepared with simple private rooms with views on spot gardens. Climbing up to the third floor via the white staircase from the side entrance of the restaurant reveals a special area for slowly enjoying a fine selection of spirits and cigars. Overall, this eatery stands out of for its dignified appearance in this quiet area of Aoyama.

穏やかな時が流れる温かな和空間

青山246通り沿いから梅窓院の竹林の小道を入った奥にある3階建ての一軒家。水が流れる1階の細い袋小路を入ると、漆の壁をバックにしたカウンターとテーブル席が。2階には坪庭の見えるシンプルな個室を用意。店舗横の入口より白い階段室を上がって3階を訪れると、厳選したお酒とシガーを吸えるゆったりとした特別空間も。青山の閑静なエリアに凛とした佇まいが印象的な一店。

1

1　The facade
2　The lacquered counter back
3　The sound of flowing water can be heard from the entrance
4　Small rise seat with a views on spot garden

1　ファサード
2　漆のカウンターバック
3　水の音が聞こえるエントランス
4　坪庭が見える小上がり席

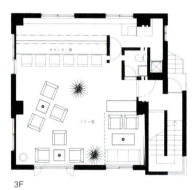

3F

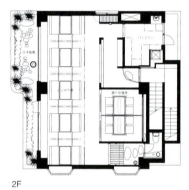

2F

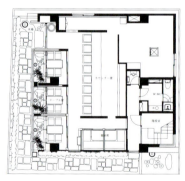

1F

KAGURAZAKA SHUN AOYAMA

Opening Hours:Lunch12:00~15:00 Dinner17:00~23:00(L.O.22:00)Lounge19:00~2:30(L.O.2:00)Holidays:Irregular Tel:03-3479-0770 Customer:30s-60s Floor Space:283.1㎡ Seats:67(counter 8, tables 12, 2rooms for4, heated tables 8, parlors20, 3F 15) Opened:23/4/2005 Operated by:aya-shoji Inc. Design:Kamiya Design Inc. Contractor:IDA INC. Cooperator:Illumination:KOIZUMI LIGHTING TECHNOLOGY CORP Lacquer tree art:Yui Higashibata, Special order illumination:WATTS Photographs:Masahiro Ishibashi

神楽坂SHUN 青山

営業時間:ランチ12:00～15:00 ディナー17:00～23:00（L.O.22:00）ラウンジ19:00～翌2:30（L.O.翌2:00）定休日:不定休 Tel:03-3479-0770 来客者層:30代～60代 店舗面積:283.1㎡ 席数:67席（カウンター8席，テーブル12席，個室(2部屋)4席，掘り炬燵8席，小上がり20席，3階15席）開店日:2005年4月23日 経営:文商事㈱ 設計:㈱神谷デザイン事務所 施工:㈱アイ・ディー・エー 協力:照明:コイズミ照明㈱ 漆芸:東端 唯 特注照明:㈱ワッツ 撮影:石橋 マサヒロ

GINZA YANOICHI

下町和食とうまい魚 銀座やの一

☐ Address：Taiyo Building7F, 8-8-5, Ginza, Chuo-ku, Tokyo
☐ Design ：C.D.C. / Akihiko Miura

☐ 住所 ：東京都中央区銀座8-8-5太陽ビル7F
☐ 設計 ：シーディーシー / 三浦 章彦

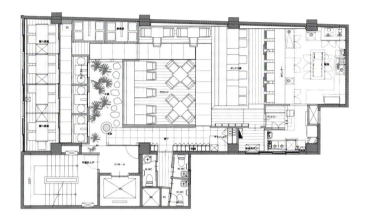

A warm and spacious presentation tucked away within a building

Located facing the main street of Ginza 8-chome, perhaps the most high class shopping district in Japan, this modern expression of an Edo period shitamachi neighborhood is a dining space that caters mainly to adults who are discerning about the ingredients used in their food. In just one space, this restaurant features a lounge, counter seating, and horigotatsu style seating, all of which are cozy and relaxing. Emphasis is placed on intimacy for the elevated seating surrounding the garden and couple seats. The ceiling is extremely low, so lighting has been installed in the floor to naturally attract guests' gazes downward.

ビルイン店舗の開放感となごみ感の演出

日本一の高級繁華街、中央区銀座8丁目のメインストリートに面した立地に「江戸・下町」を現代的に表現し、料理の素材にこだわった大人向けの衣食空間。店内は、ラウンジ・カウンター席・掘ごたつ風BOX席を1つの空間に配置して、それぞれに心地良いなごみ感を持たせている。中庭を挟んだ小上がり席・カップル席は、「こもり感」を重視。天井が極端に低い為、床に照明を仕込んで目線を自然と下げる工夫も見られる。

1

1　The counter seating as seen from the entrance   1　入口から見たカウンター席

2　Impressive silhouettes of intricate Edo patterns are found on the walls of the main floor

3　A four-person private room

4　A separated horigotatsu-style private room

2　メインフロア壁面に施した江戸小紋のシルエットが印象的

3　4名様個室

4　離れの掘り炬燵式個室

GINZA YANOICHI

Opening Hours:Weekday 17:30~4:00 Saturday17:30~23:30 Sunday 16:00~23:30 Holidays:None Tel:03-5568-7711 Customer:Late 20s OL, 30s-50s Office Worker Floor Space:164.5㎡ Seats:74 Opened:1/12/2005 Operated by:ICHINOYA Design:C.D.C. Contractor:DAISHIN KOUGEI Cooperator:HOSHIZAKI TOKYO

下町和食とうまい魚 銀座やのー

営業時間:平日17:30~翌4:00 土17:30~23:30 日16:00~23:30 定休日:無休 Tel:03-5568-7711 来客者層:20代後半OL、30代~50代サラリーマン 店舗面積:164.5㎡ 席数:74席 開店日:2005年12月1日 経営:㈲一の屋 設計:シーディーシー 施工:大信工芸㈱ 協力:ホシザキ東京

TRATTORIA AOYAMA WAINARI

TRATTORIA AOYAMA和伊也

☐ Address：Black Aoyama Building2F, 3-2-7, Minami-Aoyama, Minato-ku, Tokyo
☐ Design ：CELL DESIGN / Yuichiro Amauchi

☐ 住所　：東京都港区南青山3-2-7 ブラック青山ビル2F
☐ 設計　：㈲セルデザイン / 天内 裕一郎

A simple and modern design calculated to appeal to a female clientele

As tastes change with the times, the owner of this establishment hoped that it could be patronized in a lighthearted way, and asked that renovations turn it into a more casual destination. The previous theme was a fusion of Japanese and Western tastes, and the place had the feel of a bar, but the refit saw it transformed into a casual and simple space emphasizing the feel of a bright cafe in the hope of attracting more female customers. The facade was previously made from wood, but was reconstructed in silver, neatly expressing the simple and modern concept behind the refit.

女性客にアピールするシンプルモダンの意匠

世の中の嗜好が変化する中、より気軽に利用して欲しいとのオーナーの希望のもと、カジュアルなデザインへリニューアル。以前は「和と洋の融合」というテーマでバー的な雰囲気だったが、今回は軽快なシンプルさを強調した明るいカフェ風のデザインで、女性客にアピールしている。特に、ファサードは以前の木目調からシルバーの造作物にし、よりシンプルモダンのコンセプトを全面に出した。

1　The repetition of a circular motif defines the distinctive facade here
2　The counter and a wall that doubles up as storage for wine
3　Window-side seating featuring a circular screen with an SUS finish
4　A panoramic view of the interior

1　円の連続性のデザインが印象的なファサード
2　ワインのストック場ともなる壁面とカウンター席を見る
3　目隠しとなる丸型SUSの仕切りをつけた窓側席
4　店内全景

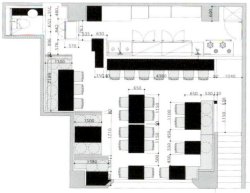

TRATTORIA AOYAMA WAINARI

Opening Hours:11:30~2:00 Holidays:Sunday and National Holiday Tel:03-3478-1417
Customer:Late20s-Early40s men and women Floor Space:58㎡ Seats:38(include couter7)
Renewal:30/3/2006 Operated by:TRATTORIA PLAN Design:CELL DESIGN Contractor:SEIKEN
Photographs:Masashi Tanaka

TRATTORIA AOYAMA和伊也

営業時間:11:30〜翌2:00 定休日:日・祝 Tel:03-3478-1417 来客者層:20代後半〜40代前半 男女 店
舗面積:58㎡ 席数:38席(内カウンター7席)改装日:2006年3月30日 経営:㈲トラットリアプラン 設計:㈲
セルデザイン 施工:㈲セイケン 撮影:田中 昌

TEKE TEKE

てけてけ

☐ Address：Matsumoto Heights B1F , 3-1, Kagurazaka, Shinjuku-ku, Tokyo
☐ Design ：LESC / Sadahito Inai

☐ 住所　：東京都新宿区神楽坂3-1 松本ハイツB1F
☐ 設計　：レスク㈱ / 稲飯 貞仁

Basement restaurant's enclosed feel banished through design

This chicken restaurant is located on the packed Kagurazaka strip in Tokyo's Shinjuku district. When patrons enter the establishment, the staff leads them inside and watches as their charges marvel at the interior. The counter seating area features a sunken wall comprised of over 110 overlapping boards which let through light and replicate the look of a chicken wing. The design incorporates many fun features, including a glass panel in the ceiling which is filled with a small garden. Besides the counter area, all the seating here is in private rooms, so in order to relieve the cramped atmosphere blocks punctuated with holes and plants are used as vague interruption which add depth to the space.

閉塞感を和らげた地下空間の鶏料理店

神楽坂軽子坂沿いの店。客が店内に入るとスタッフが客を、客が店内を見渡せ、高揚感が煽られる。カウンター席は下がり壁に100枚程の板を重ね貼りにして照明を入れ、鶏の羽を模して軽やかに。天板はガラスにして中に坪庭を組み込む等、遊び心を盛り込んでいる。カウンター以外全て個室席の為、窮屈な雰囲気にならぬよう穴あきブロックや植栽で曖昧に遮り、空間に奥行き感が感じられる。

1 The pathway into the interior as seen from the entrance
2 The counter seating to the right of the entrance
3 One of the private rooms

1 入口より店内通路を見る
2 入口右手のカウンター席
3 個室

TEKE TEKE

Opening Hours:17:00~23:30 Holidays:None Tel:03-5261-5870 Customer:30s- 50s
Female office worker, office worker Floor Space:174㎡ Seats:84 Opened:11/2005
Operated by:United & Collective Co., Ltd. Design:LESC Contractor:LESC
Photographs:Sadahito Inai

てけてけ

営業時間:17:00~23:30 定休日:無休 Tel:03-5261-5870 来客者層:30代～50代OL,
サラリーマン 店舗面積:174㎡ 席数:84席 開店日:2005年11月 経営:ユナイテッド&コレ
クティブ㈱ 設計:レスク㈱ 施工:レスク㈱ 撮影:稲飯 貞仁

070 | PUBS
居酒屋&ダイニングバー

Japanese dishes &
nabe cuisine
和食ベースの創作料理
＆鍋料理

HYO-TEI

西麻布 表邸

☐ Address ：1-5-18, Nishi-azabu, Minato-ku, Tokyo
☐ Design ：SPINIFEX / Yuki Tomosugi

☐ 住所 ：東京都港区西麻布1-5-18
☐ 設計 ：スピニフェックス / 友杉 有紀

Design that reflects the spirit of this eatery's pursuit of the essence of quality food

Nishiazabu HYO-TEI, which entertains guests with a variety of mainly Japanese dishes and nabe cuisine, is the first Tokyo location of a chain that Access-Net inc. manages restaurants in Kyushu. The food, service, and interior have all been designed as expressions of this establishment's simple and honest pursuit of quality. Excessive decoration has been avoided where possible, while the three floors of the restaurant have each been created as clearly defined separate areas through the use of basic features of space and materials. The result is a relaxing interior that compliments the food as guests dine.

食の本質を追求する店舗の心意気を反映したデザイン

和食ベースの品々と鍋料理を楽しめる『西麻布 表邸』は、九州で店舗展開する㈱アクセスネットの東京進出1号店だ。食・サービス・空間ともに、シンプルな中に本質を追求する店舗のテーマを空間デザインで表現。余分な装飾ははなるべく排除し、1階から3階に向けて除々に"個の領域"を明確にしつつ、領域感や素材感等の基本要素で構成した。食する時をより引き立てる和みの空間となった。

1

1 Relaxing, wooden counter seating towards the back of the first floor	1 木の素材感に心落ち着く1階奥カウンター席
2 Special rooftop seating with a view of the Mori Tower	2 森タワーを望める屋上の特別室
3 A view of the private seating	3 個室を見る

HYO-TEI

Opening Hours:Mondeay-Friday18:00~1:00 Saturday 18:00~24:00 Sunday 18:00~23:00 Holidays:None Tel:03-6406-0506 Customer:Late20s-Late30s, office worker, female office worker, celebrity Floor Space:226.6㎡ Seats:70 Opened:24/11/2005 Operated by:Access-Net inc. Design:SPINIFEX Contractor:Hattori Cooperator:Binhex Illumination:JAPAN LIGHTING Co., Ltd. Photographs:STUDIO B・B / Tsuguo Nishimura

西麻布 表邸

営業時間:月～金18:00～翌1:00 土18:00～24:00日18:00～23:00定休日:無休 Tel:03-6406-0506 来客者層:20代後半～30代後半 会社員, OL, 著名人 店舗面積:226.6㎡ 席数:70席 開店日:2005年11月24日 経営:㈱アクセスネット 設計:スピニフェックス 施工:ハットリ 協力:ビンヘックス 照明:ジャパンライティング 撮影:スタジオB・B／西村 次雄

Yakitori GOMITORI

伍味酉

☐ Address ： 3-6-1, Shinbashi, Minato-ku, Tokyo
☐ Design ： Guen BERTHEAU-SUZUKI Co., Ltd. / Guen BERTHEAU-SUZUKI

☐ 住所 ： 東京都港区新橋3-6-1
☐ 設計 ： ㈱玄・ベルトー・進来 / 玄・ベルトー・進来

Grilled chicken restaurant distinguishes itself from rivals through design

This venerable restaurant specializing in Nagoya Kochin chicken decided to locate itself in the Shimbashi district, famed for its many grilled chicken restaurants. In order to distinguish itself from the many competing establishments nearby, it chose the theme "Intelligent Romance" for its outfitting. The first floor features a bar, the second has table seating based around vertical lines, and the third raised seating based on horizontal lines. Having taken into consideration the endurance of materials as a unifying factor for the space as guests proceed into the space the materials graduate from metal to cedar wood. Using light iron the lighting and color scheme evokes an appealing glamour.

焼鳥激戦地に登場した新店舗の差別化

名古屋コーチンの老舗が、焼鳥激戦地の東京新橋に進出するにあたり、「インテリロマン」をキーワードに他店との差別化を図った。1階はバーフロア、2階は"縦線"からなるテーブル席、3階は"横線"からなる小上がり席に。空間の統一感として仕上材の耐久性も考慮し、外から中へ進むに従い線の材質を金属から杉板へと移行。軽鉄をそのまま使用して、照明や色彩計画により程よく色気のある空間にまとまった。

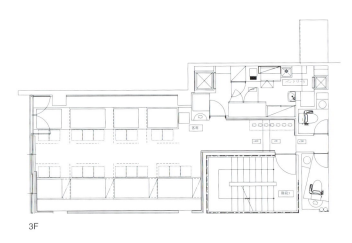

3F

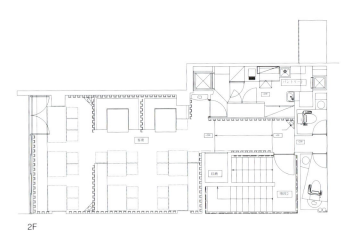

2F

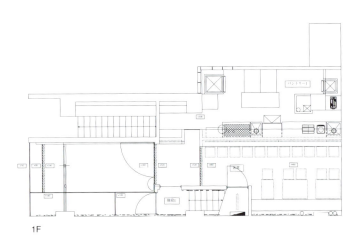

1F

1

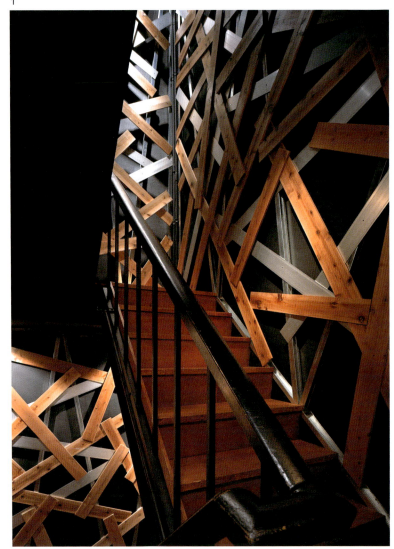

1 The lines of each floor are randomly applied to the stairs that connect them
2 The aluminum louver of the facade is also used for the ceiling of the bar

1 各階の線を階段にランダムに配し各フロアを繋げている
2 ファサードの水平アルミルーバーをバー天井にも使用

3 The second-floor table seating
4 The raised seating on the third floor

3 2階テーブル席
4 3階小上がり席

Yakitori GOMITORI

Opening Hours:Monday-Friday17:00~23:30(LO.22:30)Saturday and Sunday and National Holiday17:00~23:00(LO.22:00) Holidays:None Tel:03-5510-7872 Customer:20s-50s men and women Floor Space:251.45㎡ Seats:96 Opened:27/1/2005 Operated by:Taste Corporation Design:Guen BERTHEAU-SUZUKI Co., Ltd. Contractor:IDI PLANNING CO.,LTD. Cooperator:Iwato Consultant Photographs:Nacása & Partners inc.

伍味酉

営業時間:月～金17:00～23:30(LO.22:30)土・日・祝17:00～23:00(LO.22:00) 定休日:無休 Tel:03-5510-7872 来客者層:20代～50代の男女 店舗面積:251.45㎡ 席数:96席 開店日:2005年1月27日 経営:㈱テイスト 設計:㈱玄・ベルトー・進来 施工:㈱IDI企画 協力:侑岩戸設計コンサルタント 撮影:Nacása & Partners inc.

7　BARS

バー

Thunder Bolt

サンダーボルト

☐ Address ：Kami-Meguro-SS Building 2F Right, 1-3-19, Kami-Meguro, Meguro-ku, Tokyo

☐ Design ：YUSAKU KANESHIRO ＋ ZOKEI-SYUDAN Co., Ltd. / Yusaku Kaneshiro , Mitsuru Komatsuzaki

☐ 住所 ：東京都目黒区上目黒1-3-19 上目黒SSビル 2F右

☐ 設計 ：兼城 祐作十造形集団㈱ / 兼城 祐作・小松崎 充

Japanese-style space that plays on contrasts of strong and soft

Thunderbolt features a ceiling mural depicting dancing dragons and gods of wind and thunder, with lighting fixtures behind the counter that strengthen the overall design. Based on Japanese style, this unusual space mixes elegance with a glamorous look. The gorgeous chandelier is a focal point of the interior and crucial to the balance of strength and softness that defines the space. The name of the bar conjures up a dynamic, electric image appropriate to a space that lights up the evening of its patrons with a fabulous brilliance.

和をベースに生み出した剛と柔の絶妙なデザイン

竜神の舞う天井画と風神雷神をテーマに、オブジェ照明を施したカウンターバックを力強くデザインした『サンダーボルト』。和をベースに、雅びな世界とグラマラスな世界が混在し、独特な雰囲気を持つ。色気のあるシャンデリアがポイントとなって、全体的に剛と柔のバランスが程よく取れた空間だ。店名『サンダーボルト』＝雷のイメージが大胆に表われ、夜の闇に光彩を放つ一店。

1

1 The entrance, replete with lightning bolt motif   1 稲妻形が頭上に光るエントランス

2 The counter seating, which is dominated by the ceiling mural   2 天井画の迫力に圧倒されるカウンター席

3   The private room located in back of the establishment

3   店内奥にある個室空間

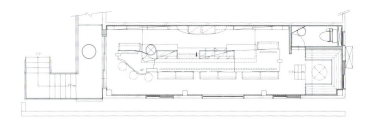

Thunder Bolt

Opening Hours:19:00~5:00 Holidays:Monday Tel:03-6666-6773 Customer:20s-40s men and women Floor Space:33㎡ Seats:21 Opened:3/3/2006 Operated by:Lupin J Hayam Design:YUSAKU KANESHIRO ＋ ZOKEI-SYUDAN Co., Ltd. Contractor:PI Architects Design Photographs:Masahiro Ishibashi

サンダーボルト

営業時間:19:00〜翌5:00 定休日:月曜 Tel:03-6666-6773 来客者層:20代〜40代男女 店舗面積:33㎡ 席数:21席 開店日:2006年3月3日 経営:ルパン J 葉山 設計:兼城 祐作十造形集団㈱ 施工:㈲ピー・アイ・建築デザイン 撮影:石橋 昌弘

073 | BARS
バー

Champagne Bar
シャンパンバー

Brumed'or

ブリュームドール

☐ Address：Duo Scala Nishi-Azabu Tower B1F, 1-2-12, Nishi-Azabu, Minato-ku, Tokyo
☐ Design ：STUDIO NAGARE Co., Ltd. / Takahiro Yokoi

☐ 住所 ：東京都港区西麻布1-2-12 デュオスカーラ西麻布タワーB1F
☐ 設計 ：㈱スタジオナガレ / 横井 貴広

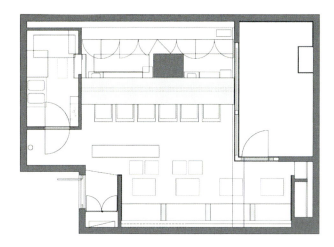

A space designed to be 'a private urban hideaway'

The design concept for this space is "A Man's Hideaway Holiday Home." In order to fire up the imagination, patterned curtains and sofas; handles made from Swarovski crystals; underwater illumination and indirect lighting are all unified by a tasteful brown color scheme. In order for a sophisticated clientele to relax to the fullest, a secret room and an aroma massage room have been incorporated into the design, allowing them more options for spending their precious time here.

"自分なりの都会の隠れ家"をイメージさせる仕掛け

デザインコンセプトは「男の隠れ家としての別荘」。イマジネーションを誘発させる仕掛けとして、柄物のカーテンやソファのパターン、スワロフスキーのクリスタルの把手等を用意し、水中照明や間接照明で引き立て、全体をブラウン系でまとめ上げた。ゆっくり寛ぎたい大人のために、シークレットルームやアロママッサージルーム等、自分に合うサービスを選択できる空間も設けられている。

1

1 The counter seating　　1 カウンター席

2

2　The table seating
3　The secret room with its sparkling chandelier

2　テーブル席
3　シャンデリアが煌めくシークレットルーム

Brumed'or

Opening Hours:Tuesday-Saturday18:00~5:00 Monday and National Holiday18:00~23:30 Holidays:Sunday Tel:03-3470-4505 Customer:20s Females, Earlry30s Office worker Floor Space:83㎡ Seats:30(counter 6, lounge14, secret booth 6~15) Opened:19/7/2005 Operated by:in the GROOVE Co., Ltd. Design:STUDIO NAGARE Co., Ltd. Contractor:Izumo Planning Photographs:Kunio Okoshi

ブリュームドール

営業時間：火～土18:00～翌5:00 月・祝18:00～23:30 定休日：日曜 Tel:03-3470-4505 来客者層：20代女性，30代前半のサラリーマン 店舗面積：83㎡ 席数：30席（カウンター6席，ラウンジ14席，シークレットブース6～15席）開店日：2005年7月19日 経営：㈱in the GROOVE 設計：㈱スタジオナガレ 施工：㈱イズモプランニング 撮影：大越 邦生

SALON TSUKIAKARI

サロン月灯り

☐ Address ：ANNEX4F , 1-23-36, Azumabashi , Sumida-ku, Tokyo
☐ Design ：Kamiya Design Inc. / Toshinori Kamiya

☐ 住所 ：東京都墨田区吾妻橋1-23-36 ANNEX 4F
☐ 設計 ：㈱神谷デザイン事務所 / 神谷 利徳

Clever use of maker-managed complex-style restaurant space

Salon Tsukiakari is the bar lounge located on the fourth floor of the Asahi Beer Annex building restaurant complex. Each floor has been designed with a different concept, with the first floor being a cafe, the second an izakaya, and the third a restaurant. A large glass skylight has been built into the roof of the fourth floor so that the light of the moon (tuskiakari in Japanese; hence the name) can shine upon the interior of the lounge. All spirits handled by Asahi Beer are available, and in the afternoon the space serves as a testing ground for new types of services where various wine schools or parent/child cocktail classes are held.

メーカー経営のコンプレックス型レストランの活用法

レストランコンプレックス型のアサヒビールANNEXビル4階のバーラウンジ。1階はカフェ、2階は居酒屋、3階はレストランとして各々のコンセプトで空間を構成。4階は天井に大きなガラストップライトが設けられ、月明りが店内に差し込む。ここにはアサヒビールが取扱う全ての酒が揃い、昼間はワインスクールや親子カクテル教室等のイベントが開催するなど、新サービスの提案の場となっている。

1

1   An entrance that promises a lively interior   1   華やかな空間を期待させるエントランス
2   The lounge   2   ラウンジ

3

4

3 Counter seating
4 The VIP Room

3 カウンター席
4 VIPルーム

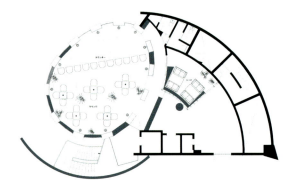

SALON TSUKIAKARI

Opening Hours:Monday-Saturday17:00~1:00(L.O.) Sunday and National Holiday17:00~24:00(L.O.) Holidays:None Tel:03-5608-3834 Customer:Over40s couples Over 30s ladies group Floor Space:203.39㎡ Seats:39(counter 11, main floor20, private rooms8 Opened:3/5/2005 Operated by:ASAHI BEER ANNEX.,LTD. Design:Kamiya Design Inc. Contractor:TEN-NEN-SHA INC. Cooperator:illumination:USHIOSPAX Lacquer tree art Yui Higashibata Special order illumination:WATTS Photographs:Keisuke Miyamoto

サロン月灯り

営業時間：月〜土17:00〜翌1:00（L.O.）日・祝17:00〜24:00（L.O.）定休日：無休 Tel:03-5608-3834 来客者層：40代以上のカップル層，30代以上の女性グループ 店舗面積:203.39㎡ 席数:39席（カウンター11席，メインフロア20席，個室8席）開店日:2005年5月3日 経営:㈱アサヒビールアネックス 設計:㈱神谷デザイン事務所 施工:㈱天然社 協力:照明:㈱ウシオスペックス 漆芸:東端 唯 特注照明:㈱ワッツ 撮影:宮本 啓介

Counter Bar TAKETSURU by AIDMA

カウンターバー 竹鶴 by AIDMA

☐ Address：Kameya-Syuhan Building 203, 1-18-3, Kamiogi, Suginami-ku, Tokyo
☐ Design ：YUSAKU KANESHIRO ＋ ZOKEI-SYUDAN Co., Ltd. / Yusaku Kaneshiro , Miho Umeda

☐ 住所　：東京都杉並区上荻1-18-3 第2亀屋酒販ビル203号室
☐ 設計　：兼城 祐作＋造形集団㈱ / 兼城 祐作・梅田 美穂

Sophisticated seductiveness captured with mirrors, objects and color

Following a rule shape, this interior features a u-shaped counter bar. The walls are draped with violet curtains, while a portion of the slatted ceiling overhead is distinguished by roses encased in glass which make for a florid highlight. Chairs in restrained tones add interest, while a symbolic light is placed in the center of the space and the surrounding walls feature shelves upon which a series of glass bottles are placed. Overall, this interior makes effective use of lighting and mirrors to evoke sense of sophisticated glamour.

ミラー、オブジェ、色で表現した大人の色気

尺形状の連なりで、コの字型に構成したカウンターバー。壁面は紫色のカーテンで覆い、カウンター天板の一部は、ガラスで密閉した中にバラの花を敷き詰めて華やかさを演出。チェアは各色を適度に入れて変化をつけている。中央には象徴的なオブジェ照明を設置し、周囲にガラスのボトル棚を連ねて配した。空間全体に適度な明暗を出し、ミラーを効果的に使った大人の色気を感じる空間。

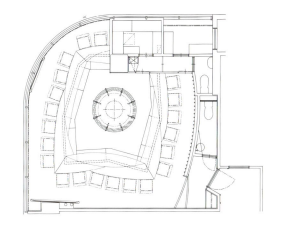

1

1　The symbolic objects are an eye-catching effect　　　1　シンボリックなオブジェが目をひく

Counter Bar TAKETSURU by AIDMA

Opening Hours:18:30~1:00 Holidays:Sunday Tel:03-3220-3690
Customer:Late 20s Office worker, Couples Floor Space:57.4㎡ Seats:21
Opened:9/3/2006 Operated by:AIDMA Co., Ltd. Design:YUSAKU
KANESHIRO + ZOKEI-SYUDAN Co., Ltd. Contractor:AIDMA Co., Ltd.
Photographs:Masahiro Ishibashi

カウンターバー 竹鶴 by AIDMA

営業時間:18:30~翌1:00 定休日:日曜 Tel:03-3220-3690 来客者層:20代
後半～ サラリーマン,カップル 店舗面積:57.4㎡ 席数:21席 開店日:2006年3
月9日 経営:アイドマ開発㈱ 設計:兼城 祐作十造形集団 施工:アイドマ開発
㈱ 撮影:石橋 昌弘

BLISS GINZA

ブリス ギンザ

☐ Address ：Ginza Miyuki-kan Building 5F, 6-5-17, Ginza, Chuo-ku, Tokyo
☐ Design ：SPOIL ASSOCIATES INC. / Shu Yamashita

☐ 住所 ：東京都中央区銀座6-5-17 銀座みゆき館ビル5F
☐ 設計 ：スポイル・アソシエイツ㈱ / 山下 秀

A counter bar at which customers get drunk on grownup conversation

The design concept here is "A Place to Spend Special Night Time." In order that customers can enjoy chatting to the bartender from any seat, two horseshoe-shaped bar counters are included in the layout. The lighting is designed to beautifully silhouette the bartender and the bottles, and makes that "Special Night Time" into an illusory experience. Also, by using only transparent materials a sparkle and that special illusory feel are emphasized throughout the space.

大人の会話に酔うバーカウンターでのひととき

デザインコンセプトは「特別な夜の時間を過ごせる場所」。全ての客がバーテンダーとの会話を楽しめるよう、2 ヵ所の馬蹄形カウンターを配置したレイアウトとなっている。バーテンダーとボトルのシルエットを美しく浮び上がらせる光の演出は、「特別な夜の時間」を幻想的なものにする。また、透明感のある素材に限定する事で、煌めきと幻想的な時間が助長されるかのように感じられる。

1　The chic entrance hall, designed for adult social interaction
2　The view of the counter seating

1　大人の社交場に相応しいシックなエントランスホール
2　カウンター席全体を見る

1

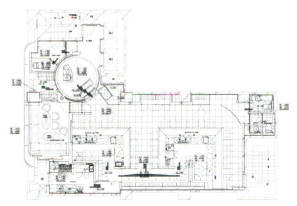

BLISS GINZA

Opening Hours:18:00 - 2:00 Holidays:Sundays and National Holidays Tel:03-3537-6721 Customer:Late 20s Males Floor Space:130.43㎡ Seats:36(counter 26, a karaoke10) Opened:6/2005 Operated by:Nomoto-Ya Co., Ltd. Design:SPOIL ASSOCIATES INC. Contractor:IDEAL Co., Ltd. Cooperator:AIDEC Co.,Ltd, USH-IOSPAX, Inc. Photographs:Nacása & Partners inc.

ブリス ギンザ

営業時間:18:00～翌2:00 定休日:日・祝 Tel:03-3537-6721 来客者層:20代後半の男性 店舗面積:130.43㎡ 席数:36席（カウンター26席、カラオケ10席） 開店日:2005年6月 経営:㈱野本屋 設計:スポイル・アソシエイツ㈱ 施工:㈱アイデアル 協力:㈱アイデック、㈱ウシオスペックス 撮影:Nacása & Partners inc.

English Pub & Foods ARROWS

イングリッシュパブ&フーズアローズ

☐ Address：Sanko Building 2F, 4-39-6, Hon-cho, Funabashi -shi, Chiba
☐ Design ：engine inc. / Takahiro Todoroki

☐ 住所　：千葉県船橋市本町4-39-6 三光ビル2F
☐ 設計　：㈲engine / 轟 貴弘

Using old wood to recreate the feel of a traditional British pub

"An Old Pub in the Backwaters of Ireland" is the theme for this interior, and an atmosphere that makes you feel a sense of history is created through the use of old wood. The wood used for the walls and other surfaces have been subjected to an aging treatment, while chandeliers and pendant lighting are created from old jars. The light emanating from the spherical chandelier made from blue jugs creates this atmosphere. Because the establishment is located on the second floor, rib siding painted with a specially mixed shade of blue, old wood and bracket lighting are used to add impact to the facade.

古材を生かして英国の古き良き伝統のパブを再現

「アイルランドの片田舎にあるアイリッシュパブ」をテーマとし、歴史を感じさせる雰囲気を出すよう古材を使用した。壁等はエイジング塗装を施し、シャンデリアやペンダント照明には古瓶を利用。薄いブルーの瓶から洩れるシャンデリア球の明りが雰囲気を作る。物件が2階であるため、特注色のブルーのリブサイディングに古材と大きなブラケット照明で、ファサードにインパクトを与えた。

1

2

1 The façade

2 The staircase at the entrance

3 The Irish-style pub space as viewed from the entrance

1 ファサード

2 入口階段

3 入口目前のアイリッシュパブスペース

4

4 The counter as seen from the Irish-style pub space
5 The English-style pub lounge space at the back of the establishment

4 アイリッシュパブスペースから見たカウンター席
5 店内奥イングリッシュパブラウンジ

5

English Pub & Foods ARROWS

Opening Hours:Monday-Saturday18:00~5:00 Sunday and National Holiday18:00~3:00 Holidays:None Tel:047-421-4777 Customer:all genre Floor Space:82㎡ Seats:37(Pub space 29, lounge8) Opened:8/4/2006 Operated by:ARROWS PROJECT Co., Ltd. Design:engine inc. Contractor:engine inc. Cooperator:YAMAZAKIYA MOKKO, KENT LIGHTING Photographs:Mizuho Tadokoro

イングリッシュパブ&フーズアローズ

営業時間:月〜土18:00〜翌5:00 日・祝18:00〜翌3:00 定休日:無休 Tel:047-421-4777 来客者層:オールジャンル 店舗面積:82㎡ 席数:37席(パブスペース29席, ラウンジ8席) 開店日:2006年4月8 経営:㈱ ARROWS PROJECT 設計:㈲engine 施工:㈲engine 協力:山崎屋木工㈱, KENT照明 撮影:田所 瑞穂

PRIVATE LOUNGE HIROO

プライベートラウンジ広尾

☐ Address ：FLEG HIROO FUSE B1F, 1-9-19, Hiroo, Shibuya-ku, Tokyo
☐ Design ：YASUO KONDO DESIGN / Yasuo Kondo

☐ 住所 ：東京都渋谷区広尾1-9-19 FLEG HIROO FUSE B1F
☐ 設計 ：近藤康夫デザイン事務所 / 近藤 康夫

Sophisticated salon distinguished by limited guest time

Offering precious private moments to its guests, 48-square-meter Private Lounge Hiroo features a 6.7 meter-high ceiling. Three tubes, each in different materials and of differing heights, are used to add interest to the space. The highest of the rooms, room A, features layers of sand beige stone paving, while room C is distinguished by walnut walls and a series of indented shelves which house lighting. This fascinatingly illusory space feels like a place frozen in time.

限られたゲストの時を彩る大人のサロン

プライベートな時を演出する『PRIVATE LOUNGE HIROO』は、天井高6.7m、48㎡の空間に各素材と高さに変化をつけ、3本のチューブを設けている。最も高さのあるルームAにはサンドラベージュの割石を積み上げ、ウォールナットの壁面を持つルームCは並んだニッチ棚に照明の役割を担う連続する配列とした。時間が止まったかのような錯覚を与える不思議な空間。

1 Room A
2 Room B
3 Room C

1 ルームA
2 ルームB
3 ルームC

PRIVATE LOUNGE HIROO

Opening Hours:20:00~midnight Holidays:Sunday and National Holidays Tel:03-5798-3156 Customer:Adults knowing play Floor Space:88.18㎡ Seats:33 Opened:3/8/2005 Operated by:FAPS Co., Ltd. Design:YASUO KONDO DESIGN Contractor:DAM.INTFRNATIONAL Cooperator:Produce:TRAIN Corporation Interior decoration execution cooperation:TABE KOUGEI Sound facilities:WAKABAYASHI ACOUSTIC DESIGN CORP. Illumination plan:n2 PLANNING OFFICE OF LIGHTING

プライベートラウンジ広尾

営業時間:20:00~深夜 定休日:日・祝 Tel:03-5798-3156 来客者層:遊びを知る大人の方々 店舗面積:88.18㎡ 席数:33席 開店日:2005年8月3日 経営:㈱ファブス 設計:近藤康夫デザイン事務所 施工:㈱ダム・インターナショナル 協力:プロデュースTRAIN Corporation 内装施工協力:田部工藝 音響設備:若林音響 照明計画:n2 PLANNING OFFICE OF LIGHTING

amebar

アメーバー

- ☐ Address ： Dogenzaka Plaza Nishinaya Building 3F, 1-18-8, Dogenzaka, Shibuya-ku, Tokyo
- ☐ Design ： Fantastic Design Works.inc / Katsunori Suzuki
- ☐ 住所 ：東京都渋谷区道玄坂1-18-8 道玄坂プラザ仁科屋ビル3F
- ☐ 設計 ：㈲ファンタスティック デザイン ワークス / 鈴木 克典

The softness and warmth born of a dark color scheme and faint lighting

The classic-looking bar's most distinctive feature is an array of oil candles. It is a sophisticated hide-away located on the third floor of a building near to the Mark City development in Tokyo's youth culture Mecca of Shibuya. The contrast and harmony evoked by the juxtaposition of bricks painted jet black with marble and rosewood provides the basis of the design, which conjures up a Scandinavian mood with its simple and modern atmosphere matched with general warmth. Overall, amebar is a sophisticated space where time can be spent at a leisurely pace.

ダークな色調にほのかに浮かぶ光の優しさと温もり

オイルキャンドルが印象的な正統派バー『amebar』。渋谷の道玄坂横、渋谷マークシティ近くのビル3階に静かに存在する大人の隠れ家だ。真っ黒に塗られたレンガの壁やブラウンの大理石とローズウッドによる"対比"と"調和"をベースにした店内は、北欧のムードを感じさせるシンプルかつモダンな雰囲気と温かみを持ち合わせる。ゆったりとした時を愉しめる上品な空間となっている。

1

3

1   The entrance
2   The counter as viewed from the table seating area
3   The table seating area

1   エントランスを見る
2   テーブル席よりカウンター席を見る
3   テーブル席を見る

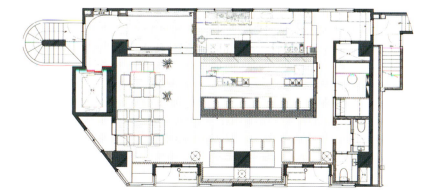

amebar

Opening Hours:18.00~2.00 Holidays:Sunday and National Holiday Tel:03-3770-
0750 Customer:20s-30s Floor Space:134.4㎡ Seats:34 Opened:19/8/2005
Operated by:Start Works Design:Fantastic Design Works.inc Contractor:DAISHIN
KOUGEI Photographs:Nacása & Partners inc.

アメーバー

営業時間:18:00~翌2:00 定休日:日・祝 Tel:03-3770-0750 来客者層:20代~
30代 店舗面積:134.4㎡ 席数:34席 開店日:2005年8月19日 経営:㈱スタートワー
クス 設計:㈲ファンタスティック デザイン ワークス 施工:大信工芸㈱ 撮影:Nacása
& Partners inc.

GINZA S

ギンザ エス

☐ Address ：Kaito Building B2F, 7-5-4, Ginza, Chuo-ku, Tokyo
☐ Design ：Synchronicity Co., Ltd. / Akira Kado , Masashi Otsuki

☐ 住所 ：東京都中央区銀座7-5-4 海東ビルB2F
☐ 設計 ：㈱シンクロニシティ / 角 章・大月 真司

Attractive space created from a fusion of contrasting elements

Located in the basement of a building on Ginza's famous Namiki Street, the initial in the name Ginza S is derived from the word "simple," which symbolizes the design's intention to allow patrons to feel at home in the space. In an area where many similar establishments are located, the theme here was a "captivating" space where customers could have fun in a sophisticated manner. Fusion the keyword underpinning the design, and the extensive use of oak to evoke an authentic ambience is contrasted with inorganic materials like mirrors and stainless steel used for fittings. The harmonious integration of contrasting Japanese and Western aesthetics, and organic and inorganic materials is the key to this interior's attraction.

相対する要素を融合して創出した妖艶な空間

銀座並木通り沿いのビル地下2階にある『GINZA S』。"好きに寛ぐSimpleな店に"とイニシャル「S」を店名に。周辺に同様な店が多い中、大人が気軽に遊べる「艶のある空間」をテーマとした。「融合」をキーワードに、オーク材を主としたオーセンティックな雰囲気を基軸とし、ミラーやステンレス等無機質な素材を付帯。「和と洋」、「有機と無機」と相対する物の調和が魅力の空間。

1

1　The table seating area is pervaded with a laidback vibe
2　The counter seating area with specially designed one-armed chairs

1　ほっとした寛ぎ感に包まれるテーブル席
2　片肘掛けのオリジナルチェアをセットしたカウンター席

3

3 The private rooms are steeped in a sophisticated atmosphere

3 非日常の時と空間が包む個室

GINZA S

Opening Hours:18:00~3:00 Holidays:Sunday and National Holiday TEL:03-3573-5074 Customer:40s men Floor Space:50㎡ Seats:counter 8, tables4~5, private rooms6~7 Opened:1/10/2005 Operated by:Yasuharu Mizota Design:Synchronicity Co., Ltd. Contractor:ART PROJECT Photographs:JPA Shooting

ギンザ エス

営業時間:18:00～翌3:00 定休日:日・祝 TEL:03-3573-5074 来客者層:40代男性 店舗面積:50㎡ 席数:カウンター8席、テーブル4～5名、個室6～7名 開店日:2005年 10月1日 経営:溝田 靖治 設計:㈱シンクロニシティ 施工:㈱アートプロジェクト 撮影: JPAシューティング

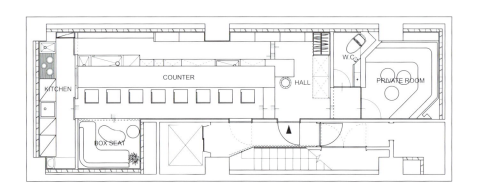

8　OTHERS

各国・各種料理

NEW YORK GRAND KITCHEN

ニューヨークグランドキッチン

☐ Address ：Queen's Square[Atto!]Station Core B3F, 2-3-4, Minatomirai, Nishi-ku, Yokohama,Kanagawa
☐ Design ：RIC DESIGN inc. / Teruhisa Matsumoto, Reiko Tanaka
☐ 住所 ：神奈川県横浜市西区みなとみらい2-3-4クイーンズスクエア横浜［アット!］
ステーションコアB3F
☐ 設計 ：㈱リックデザイン / 松本 晃尚・田中 礼子

Space design with a sense of communality that has its roots in the scenery of city

This restaurant is located in an underground shopping mall connected to Minatomirai Station. The theme is "stylish dining for adults". One of the design points is how the establishment appears from the escalators with their nonstop flow of people, so its roof is designed as a reproduction of Manhattan scenery in order to attract the eyes of passers by. As a place meant to be busy from morning until night, this restaurant has become a charming space connecting the train terminal and the shopping zone.

都市の風景づくりに繋がる公共性のある空間デザイン

みなとみらい駅直結の商業施設内地下にある店舗。テーマは「大人のスタイリッシュダイニング」。人の流動が最も多いエスカレーターからの見え方をデザインポイントとするため、屋根にマンハッタンの風景を写して移動する人々の視線を捉える。朝から昼、夜までと人の賑わいと語らいの場を提案する店舗は、ターミナルとショッピングゾーンを繋ぐ魅力的な空間となった。

1

1　The sign and logo on the facade make in impact

2　The main dining area uses red brick in keeping with the image of Yokohama

1　ロゴサインがインパクトを与えるファサード

2　横浜のイメージと繋がるレンガを用いたメインダイニング

NEW YORK GRAND

GRAND KITCHEN

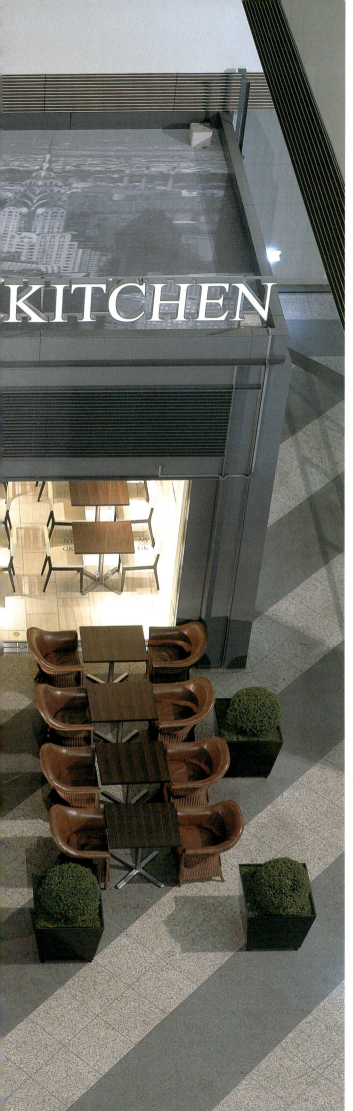

3 Photographs of Manhattan scenery as seen from the escalators
4 Indoor sofa-style seating where diners can enjoy grilled dishes and beer from nearly twenty different nations

3 エスカレーターよりマンハッタンの風景写真を見る
4 約20ヵ国のビールとグリルを楽しめる店内のソファ席

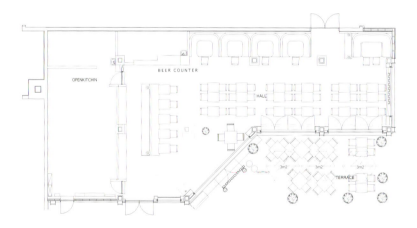

NEW YORK GRAND KITCHEN

Opening Hours:11:00～23:00 Holidays:Irregular Tel:045-226-0733
Customer:young people, young adult, couple Floor Space:231㎡ Seats:112
Opened:16/12/2005 Operated by:create restaurants inc. Design:RIC DESIGN
inc. Contractor:Tennensha Inc. Photographs:Nacása & Partners inc.

ニューヨークグランドキッチン

営業時間:11:00～23:00 定休日:不定休 Tel:045-226-0733 来客者層:ヤング, ヤ
ングアダルト層, カップル 店舗面積:231㎡ 席数:112席 開店日:2005年12月16日
経営:㈱クリエイト・レストランツ 設計:㈱リックデザイン 施工:㈱天然社 撮影:Nacása
& Partners inc.

PETIT FOUR CAFE ERABLE

プチフールカフェ エラブル

☐ Address ：La Pale Kasuga1F, 2-10-8, Kasuga, Chuo-ku, Chiba-shi, Chiba
☐ Design ：ozi design works inc. / Ryosuke Hashimoto

☐ 住所 ：千葉県千葉市中央区春日2-10-8 ラ・ペール春日1F
☐ 設計 ：オジデザインワークス㈲ / 橋本 亮介

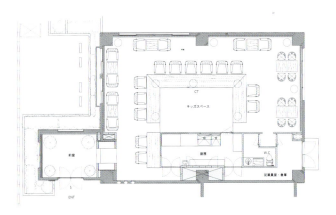

New style café where parents and their children can relax in style

Having created a play space with carpet running from the counter to the walls, this café allows mothers to watch their children frolic as they relax and enjoy the sophisticated surroundings. The interior is done out in white and beige making it very soothing, and the distinctive entrance features white pebbles and translucent curtains that add a brightness to the space. Many details, including toilets spacious enough for mother and child to use together, make this a very parent-friendly destination.

親子でゆったり寛げる新スタイルカフェ

カウンターの内側に壁面までカーペットを敷き詰めたプレイスペースを作り、子供たちが遊ぶのを眺めつつ母親もお洒落な空間で寛げるカフェ。店内は白とベージュで統一し、心落ち着く場となっている。特徴的なエントランスには白い砂利玉を敷き、薄いカーテンをつけて明るい空間を創出。子供と一緒に使える様にトイレを広く取る等の細かい配慮を成した、親子に優しいデザインだ。

1

1 The outside view of the facade
2 The entrance

1 ファサード夕景
2 エントランス

3

3　The play space as seen from the entrance

3　エントランスよりプレイスペースを臨む。

PETIT FOUR CAFE ERABLE

Opening Hours:9:00~19:00 Holidays:Monday, Every second and fourth Sunday
Tel:043-242-3328 Customer:20s-30s woman Floor Space:132.90㎡
Seats:30(included counter14) Opened:25/7/2005 Operated by:Tomohisa Ishikawa
Design:ozi design works inc. Contractor:soar-zoken Cooperator:KOIZUMI
SANGYO Co.,Ltd., Fujimac Co., Ltd. Photographs:Kanta Ushio

プチフールカフェ エラブル

営業時間:9:00～19:00 定休日:月曜、第2.4日曜 TEL:043-242-3328 来客者層:20代
～30代 女性 店舗面積:132.90㎡ 席数:30席（内カウンター14席） 開店日:2005年7月
25日 経営:石川 智久 設計:オジデザインワークス㈲ 施工:㈱ソアー造研 協力:小泉産業
㈱ ㈱フジマック 撮影:牛尾 幹太

Syoto Sabo

松濤茶房

□ Address ：SHIESPA 1F , 1-28-1 Shoto, Shibuya-ku, Tokyo
□ Design ：SPOIL ASSOCIATES INC. / Shu Yamashita

□ 住所 ：東京都渋谷区松濤1-28-1 シェスパ松濤1F
□ 設計 ：スポイル・アソシエイツ㈱ / 山下 秀

A pleasant space steeped in the Japanese sensibility

Despite being part of a members-only spa for women, this cafe is open to the general public. Taking into account the nature of the adjacent establishment, a Japanese look forms the basis of this pleasant, feminine interior. Rather than being a contrived approximation of Japanese style, the space uses natural materials to evoke a sense of warmth. Elegant motifs used in key places are designed to express femininity and define its positioning by the side of a spa.

和の表情が生み出す柔らかな空気感

会員制女性専用スパの一部で、一般客も利用できるカフェ。隣接する施設を考慮して和を基調とし、嫌みのない「フェミニンな空間」となっている。型にはまった和の表現ではなく、清潔感のある素材をベースに、より素材感を感じる天然素材を織り交ぜて暖かさを演出。また、アクセントとして雅なモチーフを要所に用いてより女性らしさを表現し、このスパ施設におけるポジショニングを明確にしている。

1

1　The hall as viewed from the entrance　　1　エントランスからホールを覗く

2   The view of the counter from the hall   2   ホールからカウンターを覗く

3   The sofa seating   3   ソファ席を覗く

4   The counter seating   4   カウンター席を覗く

3

4

Syoto Sabo

Opening Hours：11:00~23:00 Holidays：Irregular Tel：03-3477-2100 Customer：Over 20 Femals Floor Space：55.96㎡ Seats：40(counter 8, tables 4, terrace 20, sofa 8) Opened：1/2006 Operated by：UNIMAT FUTURE Design：SPOIL ASSOCIATES INC. Contractor：Forme Co., Ltd. Cooperator：TAISEI CORPORATION, AIDEC Co.,Ltd, USHIOSPAX, Inc. Photographs：Nacása & Partners inc.

松濤茶房

営業時間：11:00~23:00 定休日：不定休 TEL：03-3477-2100 来客者層：20代以上の女性客 店舗面積：55.96㎡ 席数：40席（カウンター8席、テーブル席4席、テラス20席、ソファ席8席）開店日：2006年1月 経営：㈲ユニマット・フューチャー 設計：スポイル・アソシエイツ㈱ 施工：㈱フォルム /協力：大成建設㈱ ㈱アイデック ㈱ウシオスペックス 撮影：Nacása & Partners inc.

YOSHOKU MIYASHITA

洋食MIYASHITA

☐ Address ：Omotesando-hills 3F, 4-12-10 , Jingu-mae, Shibuya-ku, Tokyo
☐ Design ：Kamiya Design Inc. / Toshinori Kamiya , Hisashi Noma , Yufui Lee

☐ 住所 ：東京都渋谷区神宮前4-12-10 表参道ヒルズ3F
☐ 設計 ：㈱神谷デザイン事務所 / 神谷 利徳・野間 久・李 悠希

A new style and interior born from the fusion of Japanese and western sensibilities

Yoshoku Miyashita is a Western-style eatery opened within Omotesando Hills by Kurayamizaka Miyashita. They offering here is of arrangements of Japanese materials along with articles that bring about a suitable sense of depth. The interior is a random mixture of varnished walls and shaved wood ceiling designs that create roughness and accentuate their Japanese nature. However, the overall atmosphere is that of a Western restaurant. The open kitchen at the entrance features a line-up of various sauces such as those used in pot-au-feu that heighten guests expectations.

和と洋の融合で生まれる新しいスタイルと空間

『暗闇坂 宮下』が、表参道ヒルズを舞台にオープンした洋食スタイルの店。提供するのは、和の素材アレンジに当店らしい奥行きを醸し出す品々。店内は、ランダムな組み合わせの漆の壁や天井の突板デザインで凹凸を出して和のイメージを強調しつつも、全体的に洋食の空気感が漂う。入口のオープンキッチンにはポトフ等で使用する数種のソースを並べ客の期待を高めるシズル感の効果も。

1

1　The entrance and sign as seen from the pedestrian walkway
2　Seating that features a lighting scheme utilizing the unevenness of the ceiling

1　共用通路から見るエントランスとサイン
2　天井の段差を利用した照明計画による客席

3　The finish of the wall behind the bench seating is a result of varnishing
4　A view of the seating and the etched glass hood above the oven

3　ベンチ席背景の壁の仕上げは漆によるもの
4　客席とくど上にエッチングされたガラスフードを見る

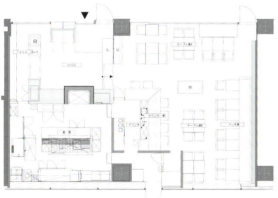

YOSHOKU MIYASHITA

Opening Hours:11:00~24:00(L.O.23:00) Holidays:Irregular (Days when Omotesando Hills is closed) Tel:03-5785-0707 Customer 30s-40s Floor Space :131.48㎡ Seats:42(counter 6, table36) Opened:11/2/2006 Operated by:D's Inc. Design:Kamiya Design Inc. Contractor:Mori Building Co.,Ltd. Cooperator:Illumination USHIOSPAX Furniture COMPLEX Special order handiwork R Inc. Photographs:Masahiro Ishibashi

洋食MIYASHITA

営業時間:11:00～24:00（L.O.23:00）定休日:不定休（表参道ヒルズに準ずる）Tel:03-5785-0707来客者層:30代～40代 店舗面積:131.48㎡ 席数:42席（カウンター6席、テーブル36席）開店日:2006年2月11日 経営:㈱ディーズ 設計:㈱神谷デザイン事務所 施工:森ビル㈱ 協力:照明㈱ウシオスペックス 家具:COMPLEX 特注製作物:㈲アール 撮影:石橋マサヒロ

holy

ホリー

☐ **Address**：2-19-8, Ebisu-Nishi, Shibuya-ku, Tokyo

☐ **Design**：Kata Inc. / Ichiro Katami, Katsunori Shigeta

☐ 住所 ： 東京都渋谷区恵比寿西2-19-8

☐ 設計 ： ㈲カタ / 形見 一郎・重田 克憲

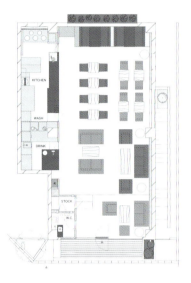

Café finds a solution to its semi-subterranean location

Situated close to Daikanyama Station, this café is situated half underground, but is designed to allow visitors to feel a sense of the outdoor air. Originally it had a low ceiling and there was a very oppressive feel in the back. By creating an aperture in back and finishing the floor, walls and ceiling all in the same material, that oppressive feel has been done away with and replaced with a relaxed and spacious feel. The simple yet modern interior allows patrons to relax in a priceless urban oasis.

半地下スペースの閉塞感を解決したカフェ

代官山駅最寄りにあるカフェ。半地下でありながらも、外の空気感を感じるシーン作りを心掛けた店舗だ。元々は、天井が低く、奥に深い圧迫感のある空間だった。そこへ、開口部が設けられ、床・壁・天井の仕上げが同一化されて圧迫感が和らぎ、落ち着きと開放感が同居する空間に仕上がった。シンプルかつモダンな寛ぎの場として、重宝される街のオアシス。

1

2

1 The facade
2 The entrance
3 The interior as seen from the entrance

1 ファサード
2 入口
3 入口より店内を見る

5

4 The newly inserted window, through the fire escape staircase is visible
5 The bench seating at the back of the café

4 非常階段が覗く嵌めごろし窓
5 店内奥のベンチシート

holy

Opening Hours:11:00~midnight Holidays:Wednesday Tel:03-5456-3363
Customer:30s men and women Floor Space:90.58㎡(terrace9.62㎡) Seats:36
Opened:30/9/2005 Operated by:Baroq'ue Inc. Design:Kata Inc. Contractor:TAK-
ISHIN Co., Ltd. Photographs:Risaku Suzuki

ホリー

営業時間:11:00〜深夜迄 定休日:水曜 TEL:03-5456-3363 来客者層:30代の男女 店
舗面積:90.58㎡ 席数:36席 開店日:2005年9月30日 経営:㈲Baroq'ue 設計:㈲カタ 施
工:㈱滝新 撮影:鈴木 理策

086 | OTHERS
各国・各種料理

Wine Shop &
Brasserie Bar
ワインショップ&
ブラッセリーバー

BISTY'S WINE SHOP &BRASSERIE BAR

ビスティーズ ワインショップ&ブラッセリーバー

☐ Address：Omotesando Hills B3F, 4-12-10, Jingumae, Shibuya-ku, Tokyo
☐ Design：NOMURA Co., Ltd. / Toshiyuki Taya

☐ 住所　：東京都渋谷区神宮前4-12-10 表参道ヒルズ本館B3F
☐ 設計　：㈱乃村工藝社 / 田谷 利之

A wine specialist shop that allows guests to buy and drink at the same time

This shop features nearly eighty different varieties of wine that can be tasted freely using the prepaid card style vine dispensers affixed to the walls. Making it a point to cater to various needs during business hours, the shop serves a dual purpose as both a wine seller and a drinking establishment. The atmosphere of this avant-garde wine shop is uniformly that of a relaxed salon, with neither of these business aspects being emphasized over the other.

"買う・飲む"を同時に楽しむワイン専門店

壁面に設置したワインディスペンサーにより、プリペイドカード方式で約80種類のワインを自由にテイスティングしながら買うことができる店舗。営業時間内の異なるニーズへの対応をポイントに、ワインを売る「酒販店」の顔とワインを飲む「飲食店」の顔を両立。サロンのような寛いだ雰囲気で全体を統一し、どちらかを強調するのではなく曖昧に1つの店舗としてまとめた、新タイプのワインショップだ。

1

BISTY'S WINE SHOP&BRASSERIE BAR

Opening Hours:11:00~23:00 Holidays:None Tel:03-5771-4466 Customer:Over30s
Floor Space:155.33㎡ Seats:28 Opened:11/2/2006 Operated by:BIZEN-YA Corp.
Design:NOMURA Co., Ltd. Contractor:NOMURA Co., Ltd. Photographs:JPA
Shooting

ビスティーズ ワインショップ&ブラッセリーバー

営業時間:11:00〜23:00 定休日:無休 Tel:03-5771-4466
来客者層:30代以上 店舗面積:155.33㎡ 席数:28席 開店
日:2006年2月11日 経営:㈱備前屋 設計:㈱乃村工藝社
施工:㈱乃村工藝社 撮影:JPAシューティング

壁面のワインディスペンサーに約80種類のワインを設置

1　The multitude of bottles on display can be sampled in the store　　　　1　陳列した数々のボトルは店内でも味わえる

2　Nearly eighty different varieties of wine are available from the wine dispensers on the walls　　　　2　壁面のワインディスペンサーに約80種類のワインを設置

NUCHIGUSUI

沖縄料理と泡盛古酒 ぬちぐすい

☐ Address：1-20-5 , Asakusa, Taito-ku, Tokyo
☐ Design ：YUSAKU KANESHIRO + ZOKEI - SYUDAN Co., Ltd. / Yusaku Kaneshiro , Mitsuru Komatsuzaki

☐ 住所　：東京都台東区浅草1-20-5
☐ 設計　：兼城 祐作＋造形集団㈱ / 兼城 祐作・小松崎 充

2F

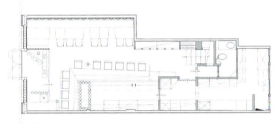

1F

1

An old time restaurant that cleverly incorporates the culture of Okinawa

Meaning "medicine of life" in the Okinawan dialect, Nuchigusui offers healthy food from Japan's southernmost islands. With Okinawa serving as the theme, lapis lazuli tiling, shiisaa and bottles of Okinawan liquor are used to capture the exotic feel of the tropical islands. On the first floor, kajumar wood pillars wrapped in vines, and the shrouded skeleton ceiling lend the space an organic feel. On the second floor, bottles covered the entire surface of the walls in the group seating area, and in all the semi-private rooms, where guests are required to remove their shoes, an even more laidback feel pervades.

沖縄に伝わる文化を巧みに取り込んだ郷土料理店

沖縄の言葉で"命の薬"を表わす『ぬちぐすい』では、体に美味しい沖縄料理を提供する。沖縄をテーマに、琉球瓦、シーサー、泡盛の瓶等の沖縄の文化素材を店内に陳列。1階は、構造柱に蔦を巻き付けてガジュマルの木に見立て、スケルトンの天井全体を覆い空間全体を有機的なものに。2階は、瓶のディスプレイが壁全面を覆う宴会席等、全て靴脱ぎの半個室空間で、より一層寛ぎ感を味わえる。

1　The first floor seating, where kajumar draws attention to the power of life
2　Neatly arranged red tiles make for a beautiful entrance

1　ガジュマルの力強い生命力を思い、畏怖をも感じる1階席
2　整然と並べられた赤瓦が美しい入口

4

3　The display shelves on the second floor where bottles of liquor are displayed

4　The showcase on the second floor in which various shiisaas are displayed

3　2階宴会席の壁面を覆う瓶のディスプレイ棚

4　様々なシーサーを飾る2階通路のショーケース

NUCHIGUSUI

Opening Hours:17:00~23:30 Holidays:None Tel:03-5828 6700 Customer:Late 20s-60s Those working in the area and living nearby Floor Space:132㎡ Seats:73(counter10, tables63) Opened:27/12/2005 Operated by:TINA'S DINNING Design:YUSAKU KANESHIRO + ZOKEI - SYUDAN Co., Ltd.Contractor:indect Co., Ltd. Photographs:Masahiro Ishibashi

沖縄料理と泡盛古酒 ぬちぐすい

営業時間:17:00～23:30 定休日:無休 TEL:03-5828-6788 来客者層:20代後半～60代 近隣の会社員及び住人 店舗面積:132㎡ 席数:73席（カウンター10席、テーブル63席） 開店日:2005年12月27日 経営:㈲ティナズダイニング 設計:兼城 祐作十造形集団㈱ 施工:㈱インデクト 撮影:石橋 昌弘

OTOGIBANASHI

お伽噺

☐ Address ：Fujikyu Building East Building No.3・B1F, 2-16-8, Minami-Ikebukuro, Toshima-ku, Tokyo
☐ Design ：Fantastic Design Works.inc / Katsunori Suzuki

☐ 住所 ：東京都豊島区南池袋2-16-8 藤久ビル東3号館 B1F
☐ 設計 ：㈲ファンタスティック デザイン ワークス / 鈴木 克典

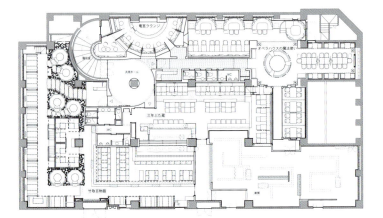

Four themes work in concert to create a veritable food theme park

Located in the food complex at the east exit of Tokyo's Ikebukuro Station, this establishment's theme is a grownup's fantasy tale. For highly individual restaurants sit side by side making for a vibrant synergy and capitalizing on economies of scale. Taketorihyakumonogatari is themed around bamboo, while Sannenbutazo is distinguished by pig-shaped lanterns. Next door Opera House Magician has a bewitching look, while Blue Lounge Ryugu boasts an illusory water feature and various modern interpretations of Chinese style. A sense of fun is evident in all of these restaurants.

4テーマが呼応するフードテーマパーク

池袋駅東口にある複合飲食施設。大人のファンタジー物語をテーマに、個性的な4店を隣り合わせ、相乗効果と作業効率を考慮した。竹林が風情漂う『竹取百物語』や豚型行灯が目をひく『三年 ぶた蔵』。妖艶な『オペラハウスの魔法使い』と幻想的な水槽を配しモダンなシノワズリを表した『ブルーラウンジ竜宮』。水槽越し等から覗き見えるような「遊び」も設けられている。

1

1 The strange gleaming white entrance appears as if from nowhere and leads down into the basement　　1 突如姿を表す白く輝く奇妙な入口より地下空間へ

3

2　平安時代の寝殿造りを思わせる『竹取百物語』
3　青森ねぶたのように大型豚灯籠を吊った『三年 ぶた蔵』

2　Taketorihyakumonogatari resembles a residence from the Heian Period
3　Sannenbutazo features pig-shaped lanterns that look like wild boars

4 The design of Opera House Magician is loosely based on "Phantom of the Opera."   4 オペラ座の怪人を題材とした『オペラハウスの魔法使い』

5 The fish tank bar Blue Lounge Ryugu is inspired by the subaquatic Dragon King Palace   5 竜宮城をイメージした水槽バー『ブルーラウンジ竜宮』

OTOGIBANASHI

Opening Hours:Taketorihyakumonogatari, Sannenbutazo, Blue Lounge Ryugu Monday-Saturday17:00~4:00 Sunday and National Holiday17:00~23:30 Opera House Magician Monday-Thursday17:00~24:00 Friday and Saturday and the day before National Holiday~4:00 Sunday and National Holiday:~23:30 Holidays:None Tel:Taketorihyakumonogatari03-3985-2191 Sannenbutazo03-3985-2192 Opera House Magician03-3985-2193 Blue Lounge Ryugu03-3985-2194 Customer:20s-30s Floor Space:698.32㎡ Seats:Taketorihyakumonogatari180, Sannenbutazo85, Opera House Magician98, Blue Lounge Ryugu20 Opened:7/7/2005 Operated by:Diamond Dining.,Co Design:Fantastic Design Works.inc Contractor:Goyokensou Photographs:Nacása & Partners inc.

お伽噺

営業時間:竹取百物語, 三年ぶた蔵, ブルーラウンジ竜宮 月～土17:00～翌4:00 日・祝17:00～23:30 オペラハウスの魔法使い 月～木17:00～24:00 金・土・祝前日～翌4:00 日・祝～23:30 定休日:無休 Tel:竹取百物語03-3985-2191 三年ぶた蔵03-3985-2192 オペラハウスの魔法使い 03-3985-2193 ブルーラウンジ竜宮03-3985-2194 来客者層:20代～30代 店舗面積:698.32㎡ 席数:竹取百物語180席, 三年ぶた蔵85席, オペラハウスの魔法使い98席, ブルーラウンジ竜宮20席 開店日:2005年7月7日 経営:㈱ダイヤモンドダイニング 設計:㈲ファンタスティック デザイン ワークス 施工:五洋建創㈱ 撮影:Nacása & Partners inc.

TORAYA CAFÉ

トラヤカフェ

☐ Address ：Omotesando Hills B1F , 4-12-10, Jingumae, Shibuya-ku, Tokyo
☐ Design ：E.P.A.Co., Ltd. / Yukiharu Takematsu

☐ 住所　：東京都渋谷区神宮前4-12-10 表参道ヒルズ本館B1F
☐ 設計　：㈲E.P.A環境変換装置建築研究所 / 武松 幸治

A soothing spiritual garden that gives rise to expressions of light

"TORAYA CAFÉ", the new brand of the long-running confectionery Toraya, uses a theme of a"shadow garden". While one draws shadows when expressing light in sketches, in contrast it becomes just as important to represent light when one wants to create a sense of shadow. The brown interior is lit by "special light" that creates a dressing of shadows and makes a good location for relaxing conversation. The wish of this cafe is for those who are living a hectic life to have a place where they can feel at ease for a time.

光の表現が生み出す心落ち着く精神の庭

老舗『とらや』の新ブランド『TORAYA CAFÉ』は「SHADOW GARDEN-影の庭-」がテーマ。デッサンで光を表現するときは影を、逆に影を感じさせる場合は光の表現が重要となる。ブラウンカラーの店内に "特別な明かり" を灯し影の装いを創り出す事で、落着きある語らいの場に。「慌ただしく生活する人々にとって、少しでも安心できる時間を過ごしてほしい」との願いが込められた。

1

1　The waiting area as seen from the entrance
2　The café space created with the image of a "garden of shadows"

1　エントランスよりウェイティングスペースを見る
2　影の庭をイメージしたカフェスペース

3 The large table towards the back is meant to be used with a counter sensibility

4 A large showcase for take-out items has been placed at the entrance of the café

3 カウンター感覚で使える店奥の大きなテーブル

4 店頭に大きく配した物販用ショーケース

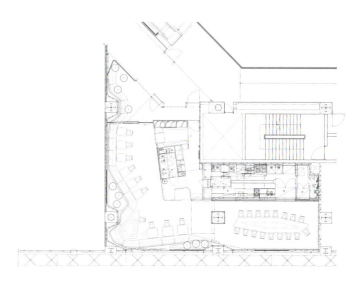

TORAYA CAFÉ

Opening Hours:11:00-23:00(L.O.22:00) Holidays:None(Days when Omotesando Hills is closed) Tel:03-5785-0533 Customer:women Floor Space:147㎡ Seats:40 Opened:11/2/2006 Operated by:Kogen Co., Ltd. Design:E.P.A.Co., Ltd. Contractor:TAKASHIMAYA SPACE CREATE Co.,LTD. Photographs:SUN-AD COMPANY LIMITED

トラヤカフェ

営業時間:11:00〜23:00(L.O.22:00) 定休日:無休(表参道ヒルズに準ずる) Tel:03-5785-0533 来客者層:女性 店舗面積:約147㎡ 席数:40席 開店日:2006年2月11日 経営:㈱虎玄 設計:㈲E.P.A環境変換装置建築研究所 施工:高島屋スペースクリエイツ㈱ 撮影:㈱サン・アド

BAR de ESPAÑA MUY

バル デ エスパーニャ ムイ

☐ Address：Tokyo Building TOKIA 2F, 2-7-3, Maunouchi, Chiyoda-ku, Tokyo
☐ Design：NOMURA Co., Ltd. / Yutaka Okuyama

☐ 住所：東京都千代田区丸の内2-7-3 東京ビルTOKIA2F
☐ 設計：㈱乃村工藝社 / 奥山 裕

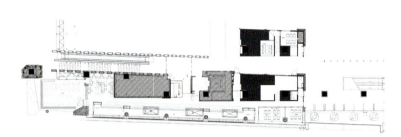

A spacious bar that makes full use of the depth and height of its interior

This establishment has been installed with a single daring counter that spans nearly thirty of its approximately 40 by 7 meter varied spread. The open counter kitchen features three hoods laid out in succession as well as wire lighting to accentuate its length. The spacious counter seating allows for communication between guests and the staff, and plays a large part in the lively atmosphere. The overall result is a restaurant where diners can eat authentic Spanish cuisine and have a casual and fun time.

空間の奥行と天井高を生かした開放感溢れるバル

約40×7mの変形した地型に、約30mの一本カウンターを大胆に設置。オープンカウンター厨房には、フードを3基連続的にレイアウトしてワイヤー照明を施し、カウンターの長さをより強調している。開放感溢れるカウンター席は、客とスタッフ、客同士にコミュニケーションをもたらし、店の活気創出に一役買っている。本格スペイン料理のカジュアルな楽しみ方を体感できる一店となった。

1

1　The drink counter in front of the register
2　The lighting behind the counter at night also catches the eye

1　レジカウンター前のドリンクカウンター
2　夜にはカウンターバックに照明が灯りアイキャッチにも

3 Private seating that makes use of the high ceiling

4 Bar seating is colored by the specially-made large pendants hanging from the ten meter high ceiling

3 高い天井高を利用した個室

4 10mの天井高を特注大型ペンタンドが彩るバル席

BAR de ESPAÑA MUY

Opening Hours:Lunch Weekday11:30~14:30(L.O.14:00)Saturday and Sunday and National Holiday11:30~16:00(L.O.15:30)Dinner Monday-Wednesday and Saturday17:30~23:00(L.O.22:30)Thursday and Friday17:30~24:00(L.O.23:00)Sunday and National Holiday 17:30~22:00(L.O.21:30) Holidays:None Tel:03-5224-6161 Customer:Female office worker, Office worker Floor Space:265㎡ Seats:120(5private rooms 26, terrace 25) Opened:11/11/2005 Operated by:GRANADA Co.,Ltd. Design:NOMURA Co., Ltd. Contractor:NOMURA Co., Ltd. Photographs:JPA Shooting

バル デ エスパーニャ ムイ

営業時間：ランチ月～金11:30～14:30（L.O.14:00）土・日・祝11:30～ 16:00（L.O.15:30）ディナー月～水・土17:30～23:00（L.O.22:30）木・金 17:30～24:00（L.O.23:00）日・祝17:30～22:00（L.O.21:30） 定休日：無休 TEL:03-5224-6161 来客者層：サラリーマン、OL 店舗面積：265㎡ 席数： 120席（個室5部屋/26席、テラス25席） 開店日：2005年11月11日 経営：㈱ グラナダ 設計：㈱乃村工藝社 施工：㈱乃村工藝社 撮影：JPAシューティング

PLANET 3rd TOKYO

プラネット サード トウキョウ

☐ Address：Tokyo Building TOKIA B1F, 2-7-3, Marunouchi, Chiyoda-ku, Tokyo
☐ Design：CAFE COMPANY INC.

☐ 住所　：東京都千代田区丸の内2-7-3 東京ビルTOKIA B1F
☐ 設計　：カフェ・カンパニー㈱

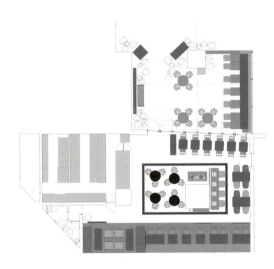

A relaxed space at the heart of Japan's most famous office district

With "House of Travel" as the concept, this interior is modeled on the home-cum-atelier of a woman named Lucy, a Chinese-European creator residing in Paris, who cherishes her Asian roots. The open and light interior with a high ceiling composed of simple materials is decorated with objects accumulated during her many jaunts across the globe, making it a comfortable, refuge-like space located at the heart of an inorganic office district.

日本を代表するオフィス街丸の内のリラックス空間

「旅の家」をコンセプトに "ルーシー" の自宅兼アトリエをイメージ。彼女は、先祖のルーツであるアジアをリスペクトするパリ在住のヨーロッパ系中国人クリエーター。この架空の設定のもと、天井が高く、シンプルな素材で構成された明るい店内には、世界で活躍する彼女が各地で収集した物とするアイテムを飾り、無機質なオフィス街に居心地良い空間を創出している。

1

1　The spacious glass entrance and terrace seating area　　1　開放的なガラス貼りのエントランスとテラス席

2 The sofa seating, done out to resemble a living room
3 The walls are used to lend the space added originality

2 リビングのような店内奥のソファ席
3 壁面のインテリア等で店のオリジナリティを演出

PLANET 3rd TOKYO

Opening Hours:Monday Wednesday, Saturday and Sunday and National Holiday11:00~23:30 Thursday and Friday 11:00~3:00 Holidays:None Tel:03-5223-8261 Customer:Local female office worker,office-worker Floor Space:138.3㎡ Seats:92 Opened:11/11/2005 Operated by:CAFE COMPANY INC. Design:CAFE COMPANY INC. Contractor:LUCKLAND CO.,LTD. Photographs:JPA Shooting

プラネット サードトウキョウ

営業時間:月～水・土・日・祝11:00～23:30 木・金11:00～翌3:00 定休日:無休 Tel:03-5223-8261 来客者層:近隣OL,サラリーマン層 店舗面積:138.3㎡ 席数:92席 開店日:2005年11月11日 経営:カフェ・カンパニー㈱ 設計:カフェ・カンパニー㈱ 施工:㈱ラックランド 撮影:JPAシューティング

Bangkok Kitchen

バンコクキッチン

Address ： Ginza corridor, 8-2, Ginza, Chuo-ku, Tokyo
Design ： Architect J Inc. / Yoshio Miyamoto, Yukiko Mizuno

住所 ： 東京都中央区銀座8-2先 銀座コリドー街
設計 ： ㈱アーキテクト・ジェイ / 宮本 義男・水野 由希子

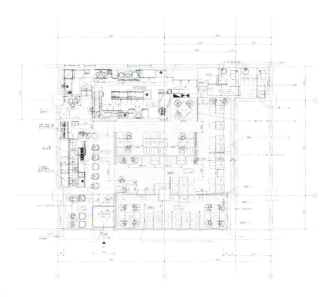

1

A stylish ethnic eatery that suits the mature mood of Ginza

This establishment offers everyday Thai cuisine to those looking to enjoy an authentic Thailand taste and atmosphere in Ginza. The design theme is a "cyberspace" in a shopping district of the avant-garde metropolis of Tokyo. The presentation is modern, using the colors and textures of Ginza's elegance. Features include white keynotes along with acrylic orb chains and lines of LED lights used to present the image of a squall. Glass partitions guarantee a moderate sense of privacy.

大人の街銀座に似合うスタイリッシュなエスニック店

銀座で本場タイの味と寛ぎを楽しんで欲しいとタイで日常親しんでいる料理を提供する店舗。デザインテーマは「先端都市、東京繁華街のサイバースペース」。銀座のエレガンスを色彩とテクスチャーを通してモダンに表現。ホワイトカラーを基調とし、アクリルの球体チェーンやLEDの光のラインでスコールのイメージを表しつつ、ガラスパーティションで適度なプライベート感も確保している。

1　The exterior makes use of steel framing with a rugged style
2　A front view of the entrance

1　ステンレスフレームに、凹凸があるタイルを使用した外観
2　エントランス正面

4

3 The acrylic counters feature Western orchids along with an effect of appearing women

4 The counter as viewed from the seating in the main dining area

3 カウンターアクリル内部に洋蘭を配し女性が映える演出も

4 客席ダイニングからカウンターを見る

Bangkok Kitchen

Opening Hours:Weekday 11:00~15:00 17:30~23:15 Saturday and Sunday and National Holiday 11:00~22:30 Holidays:None Tel:03-5537-3886 Customer:20s-30s women Floor Space:165.58㎡ Seats:79(counter5, chair seat74) Opened:27/9/2005 Operated by:Bangkok Kitchen Co., Ltd. Design:Architect J Inc. Contractor:JPD / Cooperator Graphic design:SDK / Hitoshi Takayama Photographs:SHIN PHOTO WORK Inc. / Shinji Miyamoto

バンコクキッチン

営業時間：平日11:00～15:00 17:30～23:15土・日・祝11:00～22:30 定休日：無休 Tel:03-5537-3886 来客者層:20代～30代女性 店舗面積:165.58㎡ 席数:79席（カウンター5席、イス・シート席74席） 開店日:2005年9月27日 経営：バンコクキッチン㈱ 設計：㈱アーキテクト・ジェイ 施工：㈱ジェーピーディー 協力：グラフィックデザイン SDK 高山 仁 / 撮影：㈲シンフォトワーク / 宮本 真治

093 | OTHERS
各国・各種料理

Hawaiian Dining
Restaurant
ハワイアンダイニング
レストラン

LOCO'S TABLE MAHANA

ロコズテーブル マハナ

- Address：Ginza 1-chome Building 1F ・2F, 1-15-4, Ginza, Chuo-ku, Tokyo
- Design：CA COMMAND+G / Tatsuhiro Kohge , Hideyuki Kobayashi

- 住所　：東京都中央区銀座1-15-4 銀座1丁目ビル1F ・2F
- 設計　：㈱シーエーコマンドジー / 高下 達広・小林 秀行

Gives mahana (warmth) to an office building

Situated in the heart of the upscale Ginza area, this two-floor Hawaiian-style dining restaurant features a cafe on the first floor and a restaurant on the second. The cafe level is zoned into counter and table seating with a skip floor, while the seating on the second storey was devised to cater to patrons enjoying lunch, dinner, parties and events. In a busy office district pervaded by a sense of tension, Mahana (meaning warmth in Hawaiian) is a space where one can feel the relaxed air of the famous tropical islands.

オフィスビルをMAHANA（温かさ）にする

銀座1丁目に位置し、1階はカフェスタイル、2階はレストランスタイルの2フロアで構成するハワイアンダイニングレストラン。1階はカウンター席とテーブル席をスキップフロアでゾーニング。2階はランチ、ディナー、パーティー、イベントなど多種多様な目的に対応するよう客席レイアウトに工夫をした。緊張感漂うオフィス街に、このMAHANA（温かさ）でハワイの空気感を感じてもらえる空間づくりをしている。

3

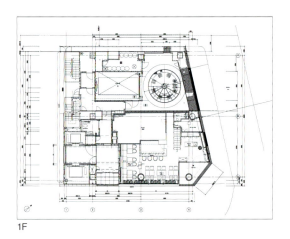

1F

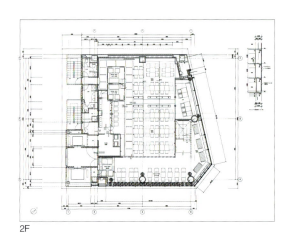

2F

1

1　Connection between the two floors is shown using round pillars and foliage on the exterior
2　The central seating area on the second floor is designed to accommodate various usages
3　The counter and table seating is noticeable even from outside

1　丸柱、植栽等で2フロアの連動感を出した外装
2　様々な目的にもフレキシブル対応できる2階中央席
3　外からの視線も意識したカウンター席とテーブル席

4 Cottage seating on the second floor gives guests the impression of being at a resort

5 The second floor sofa seating can cater to ceremonial occasions

4 リゾート感溢れる2階コテージ席

5 挙式対応できる2階ソファ席

5

LOCO'S TABLE MAHANA

Opening Hours:Weekday11:30~4:00 Saturday and Sunday and National Holiday11:30~23:00 Holidays:None Tel:03-5524-1005 Customer:20s-30s women Floor Space:1F 105.62㎡, 2F 233.59㎡ Seats:163(1F 28, 2F 135)Opened:21/7/2005 Operated by:CA FOODSERVICEco.,ltd Design:CA COMMAND + G Contractor:CA LEADING Photographs:Yutaka Nakane

ロコズテーブル マハナ

営業時間:平日 11:30～翌4:00土・日・祝11:30～23:00 定休日:無休 Tel:03-5524-1005 来客者層:20代～30代女性 店舗面積:1F 105.62㎡, 2F 233.59㎡ 席数:163席(1F 28席, 2F 135席) 開店日:2005年7月21日 経営:㈱シーエーフードサービス 設計:㈱シーエーコマンドジー 施工:㈱シーエーリーディング 撮影:中根 豊

soupcurry cocoro

スープカレー 心 中目黒店

☐ Address：FLEG Nakameguro 2F , 1-20-2, Aobadai, Meguro-ku, Tokyo
☐ Produce：Yosei Kiyono　☐ Design：YOSEI KIYONO & YO / Yosuke Karasawa

☐ 住所　：東京都目黒区青葉台1-20-2 FLEG中目黒2F
☐ 総合プロデュース：清野 燿聖　　　☐ 設計：清野 燿聖&YO / 唐沢 洋介

A design with significance for this restaurant's branch in Tokyo

This is the flagship restaurant of Sapporo-based purveyor of soup curry cocoro. The architectural composition and soft, simple design uses 360 degrees of glass walls to allow a full view of the bar and dining areas. The soft space's pendant lamps and records, and a display of books are the key features which forge the essence of the Sapporo branch into a new look for Tokyo. The small sign and lines of orange light catch the eye of people walking on the street outside and are a great way of giving the place individuality in the among the many restaurants in the Nakameguro area.

デザインが意味する東京進出店の主張と共存性

札幌発スープカレー『心』の旗艦店。建築構成とソフトに合わせたシンプルな意匠で、360度ガラス面で覆った店内は一見バーやダイニングのよう。柔らかさが漂う空間にペンダントやレコード、洋書のディスプレイをポイントに、原点の札幌店らしさを新しい形で表現した。小さなサインとオレンジの光のラインは道行く人の視線を捉え、中目黒の街で店の個性と在り方をさり気なく提示する。

1

2

1　The facade as seen from the outside　　1　ファサード全体を外部より見る
2　The entrance built into the facade　　2　ファサードエントランス方向を見る

4

3 The counter and kitchen as seen from the bench seating area

4 The bench seating as viewed from the entrance

3 ベンチ席からカウンター席、厨房方向を見る

4 エントランスからベンチ席方向を見る

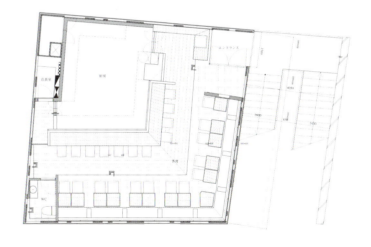

soupcurry cocoro

Opening Hours:11:00~22:00 Holidays:None Tel:03-5784-4747 Customer:20s-30s
Floor Space:80.8㎡ Seats:39 Opened:31/1/2006 Operated by:Link One Co., Ltd.
Design:YOSEI KIYONO & YO Contractor:SHIBUTANI Cooperator:MANA INTER-
NATIONAL Photographs:Nacása & Partners inc.

スープカレー 心 中目黒店

営業時間:11:00~22:00 定休日:無休 Tel:03-5784-4747 来客者層:20代~30代 店舗
面積:80.8㎡ 席数:39席 開店日:2006年1月31日 経営:㈱リンク・ワン 設計:清野 燿聖＆
YO 施工:渋谷工業㈱ 協力:㈲マナ・インターナショナル 撮影:Nacása & Partners inc.

MARCHÉ DE METRO

マルシェ ドゥ メトロ

☐ Address ：Echika Omotesando, 3-6-12, Kita-Aoyama, Minato-ku, Tokyo
☐ Design ：RIC DESIGN inc. / Teruhisa Matsumoto, Tetsuya Okabe, Miki Hashimoto

☐ 住所 ：東京都港区北青山3-6-12 Echika表参道内
☐ 設計 ：㈱リックデザイン / 松本 晃尚・岡部 哲也・橋本 美紀

Subway food court captures the feel of everyday Paris

Established as part of the recent revamp of Tokyo's Omotesando Station, Marché de Metro is themed on a Parisian market. The design uses displays of foodstuffs and a sizzling vibe created by cooking to evoke the sense of a busy Paris marketplace. Food courts are gaining popularity in Japan, and the amusing idea of recreating a piece of Paris in Tokyo is skillfully realized here by capitalizing on the buoyant mood of so many of the people passing through.

パリの日常を取り込んだ駅地下のフードコート

東京メトロ表参道駅「Echika（エチカ）」にオープンした『MARCHÉ DE METRO』。「パリのマルシェ」をテーマに、溢れんばかりの食材のディスプレイや調理するシズル感を感じさせる演出で、フランスのマルシェの日常風景を再現。新たな食のトレンドとなった都市型フードコートは、"表参道にパリを作ろう"という遊び心が上手く結実し、往来する人々が気軽に利用できる場となった。

1 Marche de Metro as seen from its entrance
2 Seating and outside light designed to resemble Parisian stalls

1 エントランスから見た『MARCHÉ DE METRO』
2 パリの街並を表現した客席と外灯

1

3

4

3　Marché is built around a circular central plaza
4　The display and open kitchen at a bakery bathed in natural light

3　円形状の広場の周りにマルシェが広がる
4　外灯越しに見るジャンフランソワ（ベーカリー）の陳列とライブ感があるオープンキッチン

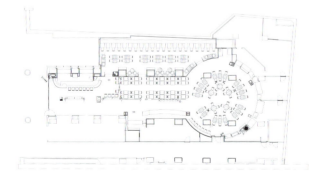

MARCHÉ DE METRO

Opening Hours:Varies by location Holidays:None Tel:03-5774-9708
Customer:Varies by location Floor Space:584.1㎡ Seats:206　Opened:2/12/2005
Operated by:create restaurants inc. Design:RIC DESIGN inc. Contractor:Hankyu
Seisakusyo Co., LTD. Photographs:Nacása & Partners inc.

MARCHÉ DE METRO

営業時間:店舗によって異なる 定休日:無休 TEL:03-5774-9708 来客者層:施設に準ず
る 店舗面積:584.1㎡ 席数:206席 開店日:2005年12月2日 経営:㈱クリエイト・レストラ
ンツ 設計:㈱リックデザイン 施工:㈱阪急製作所 撮影:Nacása & Partners inc.

CHEESE CAKE FACTORY d+c
Daikanyama, Tokyo

チーズケーキファクトリーd+c 代官山店

☐ Address：Momcheri Daikanyama 1F , 20-20, Daikanyama-cho, Shibuya-ku, Tokyo
☐ Design ：Sweetium / Tetsuo Hashizume

☐ 住所　：東京都渋谷区代官山町20-20 モンシェリー代官山1F
☐ 設計　：㈲スウィーティアム / 橋爪 哲生

Appeal of food emphasized by repetition of contrasts in shape and color

This establishment was created through the combined efforts of café and takeout store Cheese Cake factory and interior retailer Droga. The interior is arranged into three distinct sections: the takeout area; café zone and counter seating section. The design revolves around contrasts of light and darkness, organic and inorganic, hard and soft, all of which are expressed in color and form. Through the repetition of these contrasts, the deliciousness and texture of cheesecake is captured and emphasizes the individuality of a destination surrounded by competing cafes.

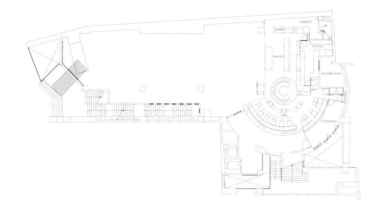

造形と色彩に"対比"を反復して主張する商品の存在感

『チーズケーキファクトリー』のカフェ&テイクアウトショップとインテリアショップ『droga』との初コラボ店。店内はテイクアウト、カフェ、カウンター席の3つのゾーンで構成。デザインは「明と暗」、「有機と無機」、「硬と軟」と"対比"を造形・色彩の中に反復させて、チーズケーキの持つ美味しさや質感を浮き彫りにし、様々なカフェ形態を生むこの街で店の個性を主張している。

1

1　A view of the four-meter-long showcase　1　4mの板ガラスを使用したショーケースを見る

2 The interior as seen from the café zone
3 The table seating in the café zone
4 The C-shaped counter appears like a piece of sculpture on the artificial glass floor

2 カフェゾーンより店内を見る
3 カフェゾーンのテーブル席を見る
4 人工芝の床上に浮かぶオブジェのようなC形カウンター席

CHEESE CAKE FACTORY d+c Daikanyama,Tokyo

Opening Hours:Monday-Thursday and Sunday and National Holiday11:30~20:00 (L.O.19:30) Friday and Saturday11:30~21:00 (L.O.20:30) Holidays:None Tel:03-3462-0566 Customer:Early 20s-30s Floor Space:104㎡ Seats:38 Opened:16/6/2005 Operated by:Cheese Cake Factory Design:Sweetium Contractor C & C PRO Co., Ltd. Cooperator:N-style Photographs:JPA Shooting

チーズケーキファクトリーd+c 代官山店

営業時間：月～木・日・祝11:30～20:00（L.O.19:30）金・土11:30～21:00（L.O.20:30）定休日：無休 Tel:03-3462-0566 来客者層：20代前半～30代前半 店舗面積：104㎡ 席数：38席 開店日：2005年6月16日 経営：㈱チーズケーキファクトリー 設計：㈲スウィーティアム 施工：㈲シーアンドシー・プロ 協力：㈱エヌスタイル 撮影：JPAシューティング

WIRED KITCHEN

ワイアード キッチン　南町田グランベリーモール店

☐ Address : GRANDBERRY MALL OASIS SQUARE1F, 3-4-1, Tsuruma, Machida-shi, Tokyo
☐ Design : CAFE COMPANY INC.

☐ 住所 ：東京都町田市鶴間3-4-1 グランベリーモールOASIS SQUARE 1F
☐ 設計 ：カフェ・カンパニー㈱

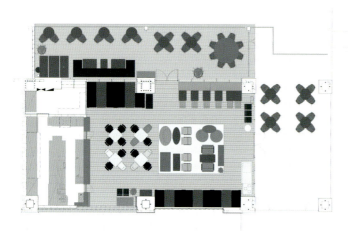

1

Suburban-style interior designed to appeal to families

The theme for this restaurant's design was "Old Hawaiian." The ceiling is high and the interior spacious, so the designers aimed for a space in which time could be spent much like as in a living room, with vintage furniture and fittings sourced from Hawaii imparting a cozy'60s feel. In order to accommodate the many families who visit this establishment with their kids, the space has been given a relaxed vibe through plentiful use of wood and the deployment of warm colors in the furniture and displays. Also, the pendant lighting in various shapes adds a pleasant accent to the simple space.

ファミリー層にアピールする郊外型店舗デザイン

『オールドハワイアン』がテーマ。天井が高く、開放的な店内は、リビングのような寛ぎ感を目指し、現地で買い付けた60年代の古き良きハワイを想わせるインテリアでまとめた。子連れのファミリー層が多い郊外のため、木の温もりを活かした落ち着きある色合いを基調とし家具やディスプレイで暖かみのある色を配している。また、様々な形のペンダント照明で、シンプルな空間にアクセントを加えた。

3

1 The glass exterior which enhances a sense of spaciousness
2 The interior, which is pervaded by a relaxed feel rather like that of a living room
3 The wood deck terrace where guests can enjoy a meal in the company of their pet dogs

1 開放感を演出するガラス貼りの外観
2 自宅のリビングのような寛ぎ感が包む店内
3 愛犬とも過ごせるウッドデッキのオープンテラス

WIRED KITCHEN

Opening Hours:11:00~23:00 Holidays:None Tel:042-796-1754 Customer:Famiry
Floor Space:149.2㎡ Seats:117 Opened:17/3/2006 Operated by:CAFE COMPA-
NY INC. Design:CAFE COMPANY INC. Contractor:MURAYAMA INC.
Photographs:Nacása & Partners inc.

ワイアード キッチン 南町田グランベリーモール店

営業時間:11:00～23:00 定休日:無休 Tel:042-796-1754 来客者層:ファミリー層 店舗
面積:149.2㎡ 席数:117席 開店日:2006年3月17日 経営:カフェ・カンパニー㈱ 設計:
カフェ・カンパニー㈱ 施工:㈱ムラヤマ 撮影:Nacása & Partners inc.

PAUL BASSETT GINZA

ポールバセット銀座

☐ Address：Ginza 646 Building1F, 6-4-6, Ginza, Chuo-ku, Tokyo
☐ Design ：spin off co., ltd. / Ichiro Shiomi , Miki Inoue

☐ 住所 ：東京都中央区銀座6-4-6 銀座646ビル1F
☐ 設計 ：スピン・オフ / 塩見 一郎・井上 美貴

A café that impresses guests with its visual and olfactory

Paul, who shined as the youngest ever barista champion, has opened an establishment that serves only the finest espresso. Using the image of the world champion and its location in Ginza as commodities, the cafe has been designed to be an overall relaxed space. In order to show the appeal of the café' specialty house roast, the interior contains various types of genuine machinery, giving it the atmosphere of a factory. The rich aroma of roasted coffee escaping from the entrances tantalizes all who pass by.

人々に視覚と嗅覚で印象づけるカフェ

史上最年少でバリスタチャンピオンに輝いたポールバセット氏が最高のエスプレッソを提供する店。世界チャンピオンによる商品イメージと、銀座という立地に合わせて全体的に落ち着きある空間に仕上げられている。店の特長である自家ローストをアピールするため、本格的な機器類で工場のような雰囲気を演出。入口を全面解放すると、焙煎したコーヒーの豊かな香りが広がり行き交う人々を刺激する。

1

1 The drink counter and the large roaster
2 A view of the interior from outside
3 The salon corner inside the shop

1 ドリンクカウンターと大型焙煎機
2 外部より店内を見る
3 店内奥のサロンコーナー

PAUL BASSETT GINZA

Opening Hours:Weekday8:00~3:00 Saturday and Sunday and National Holiday10:00~23:00 Holidays:None Tel:03-5537-0257 Floor Space:126.9㎡ Seats:26 Opened:1/20/2006 Operated by:PAUL BASSETT Co., Ltd. Design:spin off co., ltd. Contractor:union planning co., Ltd. Photographs:Shinichi Sato

ポールバセット銀座

営業時間:月～金8:00～翌3:00 土・日・祝10:00～23:00 定休日:無休 Tel:03-5537-0257 店舗面積:126.9㎡ 席数:26席 開店日:2006年1月20日 経営:㈱PAUL BASSETT 設計:スピン・オフ 施工:㈱ユニオンプランニング 撮影:佐藤 振一

DAZZLE

ダズル

☐ Address ：MIKIMOTO Ginza2 8F・9F , 2-4-12, Ginza, Chuo-ku, Tokyo
☐ Design ：ATTA Co., Ltd. / Akihide Toida

☐ 住所 ：東京都中央区銀座2-4-12 MIKIMOTO Ginza2 8F・9F
☐ 設計 ：㈲アッタ / 戸井田 晃英

The value of food and characteristics of ingredients create enchanting dining space

"Transparency" is the theme underpinning the eighth floor of this establishment. The effect is to create an optical illusion that make it seem as though one is getting lost in the kitchen, while expressing the safety of food and a sense of surprise. The ninth floor dining area makes best use of an impressive orchid-shaped window by Mikimoto, and is themed around the words "Dazzle" and "Luxury." Turning the essence of each material, including the wood used for the floor, the glass of the wine cellar and the cloth employed on the walls, this design makes for a stunning dining experience.

食の本来の価値と素材の特性で魅せるダイニング

訪れる客の目前に広がる8階キッチンのテーマは「透明性」。キッチンに迷い込んだかの錯覚を与えつつ、食の安全性とサプライズを表現。9階ダイニングは印象的なMIKIMOTOの乱形の窓を生かし、「ダズル（きらびやか）＆ラグジュアリー（贅沢）」をテーマに。木（床）、ガラス（ワインセラー）、布（壁）等各素材の美しさを本質の機能へ進化させ、鮮烈な一時を味わう空間となった。

1

1　The eight floor open kitchen, which communicates a consideration for flavor and peace of mind
2　The eighth floor bar

1　美味しさと安心への配慮が伝わる8階オープンキッチン
2　8階バーを見る

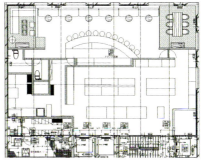

8F

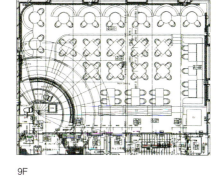

9F

3 The enormous, nine-meter-high wine cellar
4 The dining area replete with drop-like crystal decorations

3 9mに及ぶ天高に設置した巨大なワインセラー
4 雫のようなクリスタルがきらめくダイニング

DAZZLE

Opening Hours:17:30~24:00(L.O.22:30) Holidays:None Tel:03-5159-0991 Custumer:30s-
50s men and women Floor Space:392.29㎡ Seats:124 Opened:29/4/2006 Operated
by:Enterprise HUGE Co., Ltd. Design:ATTA Co., Ltd. Contractor:TEN-NEN-SHA
Cooprator:Illumination:MAXRAY.Inc.,Bup Photographs:Nacása & Partners inc.

ダズル

営業時間:17:30~24:00(L.O.22:30) 定休日:無休 Tel:03-5159-0991 来客者層:30代
~50代の男女 店舗面積:392.29㎡ 席数:124席 開店日:2006年4月29日 経営:㈱
HUGE 設計:㈲アッタ 施工:㈱天然社 協力:照明㈱マックスレイ ㈲ビーアップ 撮影:
Nacása & Partners inc.

COTTON CLUB

コットンクラブ

☐ Address：Tokyo Building TOKIA 2F , 2-7-3, Marunouchi, Chiyoda-ku, Tokyo
☐ Design ：GLAMOROUS Co., Ltd. / Yasumichi Morita, Daisuke Watanabe(EROERO)

☐ 住所　：東京都千代田区丸の内2-7-3 東京ビルTOKIA2F
☐ 設計　：㈲グラマラス / 森田 恭通・渡邉 大祐（EROERO）

1

A contemporary update for Cotton Club suited to sophisticated socializing

A place for grown-up social interaction, this space was designed as a contemporary update the hallowed original Cotton Club in the U.S. A pair of large gold chandeliers symbolizes a place for entertainment and the tinkle of crystal is a feature of the space. Brown furniture and curtains lining the walls add a sense of class and warmth and the differences in color between each of the materials lends the space a modern feel.

大人の社交場に相応しい現代版『COTTON CLUB』

アメリカの伝説となった『COTTON CLUB』の様な社交場を、現代に蘇らせるというコンセプトの基に作られた。一対の巨大なゴールドのシャンデリアには、エンターテインメントクラブを象徴するかのように、クリスタルの音符がぶら下がる。店内は、家具や壁面のカーテン等の品と温かみのあるブラウンがメインカラーとなり、各々の質感の違いから生まれる色の変化がモダンだ。

2

1　The waiting area where a mirror and curtains form a line in turn
2　The wooden flooring
3　The c-shaped sofas under the chandeliers constitutes the CLASS A seating

1　ミラーとカーテンが交互に並ぶウェイティングエリア
2　床はフローリング
3　シャンデリア下のC字ソファはCLASS A席

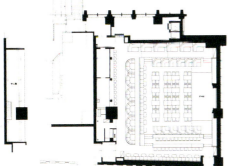

COTTON CLUB

Opening Hours:17:30~23:30 (Sunday and Holiday 16:00~23:00) Show Time 1ST 19:00 & 2ST 21:30 Holidays:None Tel:03-3215-1555 Customer:Early 30s-50s men and women Floor Space :364㎡ Seats:180 Opened:11/11/2005 Operated by:Cottonclub Japan Co., Ltd. Design:GLAMOROUS Co., Ltd. Contractor:ISHIMARU Co., Ltd Cooperator :MAXRAY Inc., Osaka Lispel Kenji Ito Photographs:Nacása & Partners inc.

コットンクラブ

営業時間:17:30~23:30（日・祝のみ16:00~23:00）ショータイム1ST 19:00 & 2ST 21:30 定休日:無休 Tel:03-3215-1555 来客者層:30代前半~50代男女 店舗面積:364㎡ 席数:180席 開店日:2005年11月22日 経営:㈱コットンクラブジャパン 設計:㈲グラマラス 施工:㈱イシマル 協力:マックスレイ㈱ 大阪リスペル / 伊藤 賢二 撮影:Nacása & Partners inc.

INDEX

The publishers and editorial team would like to extend their heartfelt thanks to all the restaurant owners, interior designers and everyone who has helped in bringing TOKYO RESTAURANT DESIGN COLLECTION 2007 to fruition. We will continue to work towards producing a guide that will be indispensable to anyone involved in restaurant design.

Publishing contents are all based on information available by September, 2006.
Wherever possible we have tried to list all information regarding the restaurants, design companies, construction companies, cooperators and photographers; any omissions are due to unobtainability.

レストラン各店のオーナー様及びスタッフの方々、経営会社ご担当者様、インテリアデザイナー様、設計会社ご担当者様など、『最新レストランの空間デザイン集 2007』の出版に際して、快くご協力いただきましたことを心より感謝いたしております。皆様に御礼申し上げますとともに、この本が、レストランデザインに関わるすべての方にとりましての一助となりますことを願って止みません。

掲載内容につきましてはすべて2006年9月までの取材情報を基にしております。
尚、店舗情報、設計・施工・協力会社名、撮影者名に関しましては明記しておりますが、不明や確認できない内容に関する表記の有無については
ご容赦いただければ幸いです。

TOKYO RESTAURANT DESIGN COLLECTION 2007

First Paperback Edition, 25/11/2006

Publisher	Yoshiaki Yanada
Publishing Agency	TENPO Co., Ltd.
Sales Agency	JAPAN PLANNING ASSOCIATION Co., Ltd. (JPA)
	3-9-12 Higashi, Shibuya-ku, Tokyo 150-0011
Sales Department	TEL.81-3-5778-7170 FAX.81-3-5766-6401
Printing and Binding	SANSHODO PRINTING Co., Ltd.
Planning and Editing	Noriko Yasuda Takako Kozakai
Shooting	Masashi Yoshikawa Saiko Sakurai Kazuhisa Yumura Masayoshi Suematsu
Design	Tomomi Wakamatsu Yoko Uchiyama
EnglishTranslation	Martin Webb

©TENPO
Printed in JAPAN
ISBN 4-88357-283-8 C2052

最新レストランの空間デザイン集　2007

TOKYO RESTAURANT DESIGN COLLECTION 2007

2006年11月25日　初版第1刷発行

発行者	梁田 義秋
発行元	株式会社テンポ
発売元	株式会社ジャパン・プランニング・アソシエーション（JPA）
	〒150-0011　東京都渋谷区東3-9-12
編集部	TEL.03-5778-7188
販売部	TEL.03-5778-7170　FAX.03-5766-6401
印刷・製本	三松堂印刷株式会社
企画・編集	安田 倫子　小堺 誉子
撮影	吉川 昌志　櫻井 彩子　湯村 和久　末松 正義
デザイン	若松 友見　内山 陽子
翻訳	マーティン・ウエブ

©TENPO
Printed in Japan
ISBN 4-88357-283-8 C2052